Fact File 2014

The facts and statistics about o

In print & online as p…

You can access the contents of this book at www.completeissues.co.uk

Your log in details:

Username: _____

Password: _____

Fact File 2014

The statistics behind the issues and controversies

Complete Issues

articles · statistics · contacts

Fact File 2014 is part of Complete Issues, a unique combination of resources in print and online.

Complete Issues

Complete Issues gives you the articles, statistics and contacts to understand the world we live in.

The unique format means that this information is available on the shelf and on the screen.

How does Complete Issues work?

Using www.completeissues.co.uk you can view individual pages from this book on screen, download, print, use on whiteboards and adapt to suit your needs. We provide you with the raw data we used to make the charts. This makes Fact File even more flexible and useful.

As well as being able to access all these statistics in PDF and raw data formats, there are references and links to other parts of Complete Issues and to the sources we used.

Fact File, Essential Articles and Key Organisations work seamlessly together on the Complete Issues website to provide you with a choice of relevant statistics, articles and contacts for further research.

Complete Issues works like a mini search engine: when you enter a topic you instantly generate a listing of relevant articles, data and organisations with a thumbnail of the page and a short description.

Your purchase of the book entitles you to use Complete Issues on one computer at a time. You can find your access codes on your covering letter or by contacting us. It is useful to record them on page 1 of this volume.

Site licences are included in all full Complete Issues subscriptions. If you are not a subscriber you can buy an unlimited site licence to make the service and the material available to **all** students and staff at **all** times, even from home.

If you do not yet have the other resources in Complete Issues (Essential Articles and Key Organisations) you can sample the service and upgrade here:

www.completeissues.co.uk

Fact File is:

Up-to-date: Revised every year using the latest statistics.

Relevant: To the UK, its education system and the concerns of young people.

Organised: Statistics are grouped within the book by theme and are cross referenced, indexed and linked on the page to closely related figures. Online searches in Complete Issues will find even more!

Attractive: Full colour and eye-catching with appealingly designed pages and great photos.

Easy to use: You don't have to worry about copyright issues as we've cleared these. Because you have both the book and online access you can use Fact File in different ways with different groups and in different locations. You can simultaneously use it in the library, in the classroom and at home.

Flexible: You can make paper copies, use a whiteboard or a computer. Different groups or individuals can use different parts of the book at the same time. Having the raw data makes it even more adaptable.

Safe: Although we have included statistics on controversial topics and tackled difficult subjects, you can be confident that students are not going to encounter inappropriate material that an internet search might generate.

Accessible: Many of our statistics come from complex reports and are difficult to understand in their original form. The attractive and clear graphical presentation makes them accessible to young people – and the use of key words online makes them easy to find.

Fact File also:

Boosts library use: Two posters are provided free with this volume. You can put one of your free posters in the library/LRC and one elsewhere – in the staff room, in a corridor, in a subject area. If you would like more copies of the poster just let us know.

Additional benefits: Subscribers to Essential Articles and Fact File are entitled to 10% discount on all our other products. They also receive occasional free posters to help promote library use, reading and study skills

Published by Carel Press Ltd

4 Hewson St, Carlisle CA2 5AU

Tel +44 (0)1228 538928, Fax 591816

office@carelpress.co.uk

www.carelpress.com
© Carel Press

Research, design and editorial team:
Jack Gregory, Anne Louise Kershaw, Debbie Maxwell, Christine A Shepherd, Chas White

Cover design: Jack Gregory & Anne Louise Kershaw

Subscriptions: Ann Batey (Manager),
Brenda Hughes, Anne Maclagan

British Library Cataloguing in Publication Data
A catalogue record for this book is available from the British Library

ISBN 978-1-905600-41-0

Printed by Finemark, Poland

FACT FILE 2014 CONTENTS

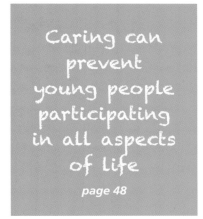

Caring can prevent young people participating in all aspects of life
page 48

Polar bears could be gone from most of their current areas within 100 years

page 74

To live a healthy life people need to be able to judge whether their own weight is healthy

page 124

23% of young drivers crashed within six months of passing their test

page 152

Alcohol advertising

Young people's views on the rules of alcohol advertising

Should it be:

- limited
- allowed
- banned?

2,362 young people under 18 from England and Wales were asked where and when alcohol should be advertised.

Most wanted stronger regulations to protect under-18s from seeing these ads.

In each case the percentage giving no answer (about 4-5%) has been omitted.

Sources and weblinks:
Source: Overexposed and overlooked, Alcohol Concern
www.alcoholconcern.org.uk

on TV it should be:

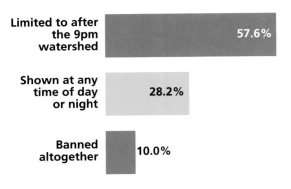

Limited to after the 9pm watershed	57.6%
Shown at any time of day or night	28.2%
Banned altogether	10.0%

in the CINEMA it should be:

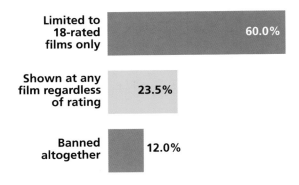

Limited to 18-rated films only	60.0%
Shown at any film regardless of rating	23.5%
Banned altogether	12.0%

> "The health warnings should be as long as the advert"
>
> *Female, aged 14*

> "Teach children earlier in school to make the right choices"
>
> *Male, aged 13*

in SUPERMARKETS AND OFF-LICENCE it should be:

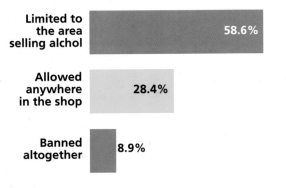

Limited to the area selling alchol	58.6%
Allowed anywhere in the shop	28.4%
Banned altogether	8.9%

> "Alcohol warnings should be visible around schools"
>
> *Male, aged 15*

on BILLBOARDS AND POSTERS it should be:

Banned near schools and playgrounds — **45.5%**

Allowed wherever they are — **28.2%**

Banned altogether — **21.9%**

on the INTERNET it should be:

Banned from websites aimed at children and young people — **60.9%**

Allowed on any website — **21.0%**

Banned from all websites — **13.6%**

Health

57.1% thought the alcohol industry should be responsible for paying for health messages about alcohol.

Only **10.1%** thought that health warnings were **NOT** needed.

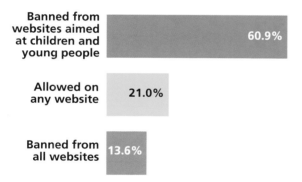

"Kids look up to sports stars and celebs – they should not advertise alcohol or wear alcohol brands on their clothing, as it encourages underage drinking"

Female, aged 15

Some issues

- Do you agree with limits to alcohol advertising?
- Is the alcohol industry or each individual person responsible for any harm from drinking?
- What else might influence the drinking habits of young people?
- Is there any other advertising that should have rules applied? Sweets? Video games?

See also Essential Articles 2014, Hey advertisers, leave our defenceless kids alone, p 127

Smoking

Smoking rates have declined dramatically, but not in all sections of society

The Opinions and Lifestyle Survey, Smoking Habits Amongst Adults, surveyed 12,620 GB adults to discover their smoking habits.

Sources and weblinks:
*Source: Opinions and lifestyle survey, smoking habits amongst adults, 2012
© Crown copyright 2013
www.ons.gov.uk*

Smoking rates, GB adults, % of individuals aged 16+ who smoke

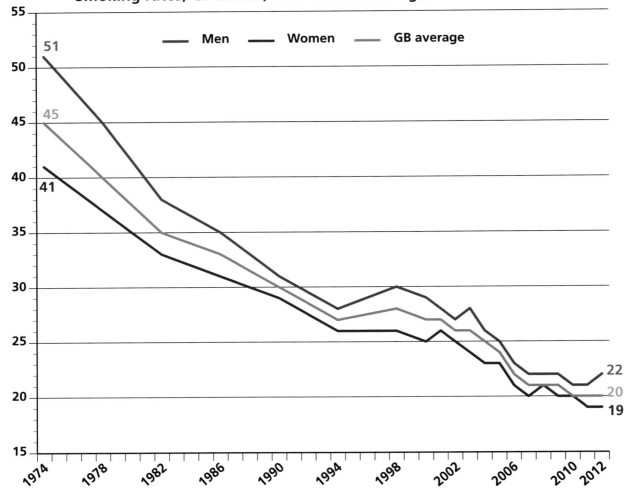

Legend: — Men — Women — GB average

Key data points: 51, 45, 41 (1974); 22, 20, 19 (2012)

There are a number of reasons that smoking numbers may have decreased. Here are a few smoking policies which might have played a role:

2006: Public smoking ban

2007: Age of sale raised from 16 to 18

2008: Printed warnings on packaging

2012: Tobacco displays banned (Wales)

GB averages may have dropped, but a closer look at the data reveals how smokers aren't distributed equally throughout British society.

While **20%** of the population as a whole are smokers, this percentage changes depending on marital status, age and whether or not you work!

33% of people who are co-habiting are smokers, compared to just **14%** of married people

29% of 20-24 year olds smoke, compared to just **13%** of people over 60

Smoking rates, % by employment status

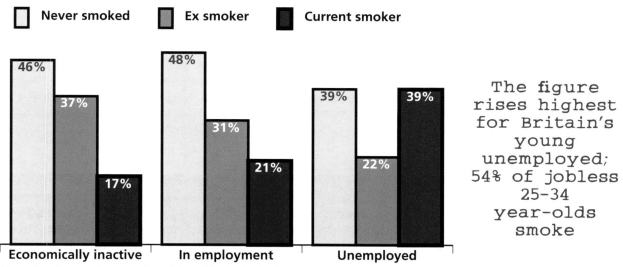

☐ **Never smoked** ☐ **Ex smoker** ■ **Current smoker**

Economically inactive: 46%, 37%, 17%
In employment: 48%, 31%, 21%
Unemployed: 39%, 22%, 39%

The figure rises highest for Britain's young unemployed; 54% of jobless 25-34 year-olds smoke

Unemployed means those wanting a job, seeking in the last four weeks and available to start in the next two.
Economically inactive means those in retirement and those who are not actively seeking work.

Recession roll-ups?

The rising price of cigarettes is probably affecting buying habits too. These days, **1 in 3 smokers** don't buy ready-made cigarettes in packets. There's a big gender difference here - **38%** of men who smoke choose roll-ups, compared to just **24%** of women.

Age is also important. If they're over 60, **81%** of female smokers buy packet cigarettes, compared to **57%** of 16 to 24 year olds.

Some issues

- What do you think is the main reason that fewer people smoke?

- How do you think marital status would affect whether or not a person smoked?

- Why do you think more young, unemployed people smoke?

e-smoking

Smoking is the leading cause of preventable death in Britain, so are more people turning to e-cigarettes? ASH (Action on Smoking and Health) reveals figures about the increasing number of e-smokers.

Are e-cigarettes the solution to smoking deaths?

Sources and weblinks:
Source: ASH - Action on Smoking and Health;
British Medical Association
www.ash.org.uk
www.bma.org.uk

SMOKING KILLS MORE THAN HALF OF ALL SMOKERS WORLDWIDE: mostly from cancer. It is the single biggest avoidable risk of premature death.

Yet there are about 30 million new smokers a year, scientists have calculated.

Cigarette companies are targetting the non-smoking populations of the developing world. According to the scientists this will mean hundreds of millions of people will be dying of cancer in the second half of this century.

SMOKING IS THE LEADING CAUSE OF PREVENTABLE ILLNESS AND PREMATURE DEATH IN GREAT BRITAIN: Reducing smoking has been a key objective of Government policy on improving health.

ONE NEW DEVICE TO HELP IS THE E-CIGARETTE: These are battery-operated products which look like conventional cigarettes. They allow people to behave as if they are smoking without the most harmful effects. Some e-cigarettes deliver a dose of nicotine, which is addictive, but they don't contain the harmful chemicals that smoking tobacco does.

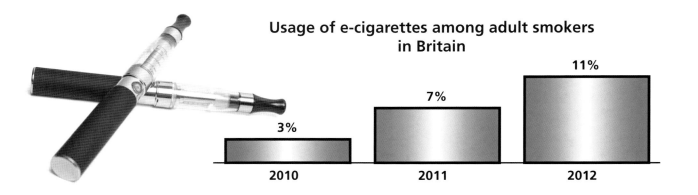

Usage of e-cigarettes among adult smokers in Britain

- 2010: 3%
- 2011: 7%
- 2012: 11%

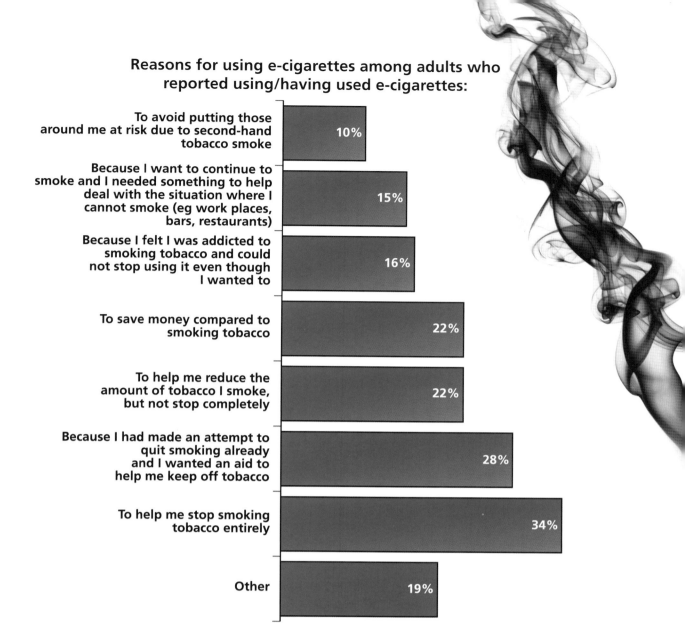

Reasons for using e-cigarettes among adults who reported using/having used e-cigarettes:

To avoid putting those around me at risk due to second-hand tobacco smoke — 10%

Because I want to continue to smoke and I needed something to help deal with the situation where I cannot smoke (eg work places, bars, restaurants) — 15%

Because I felt I was addicted to smoking tobacco and could not stop using it even though I wanted to — 16%

To save money compared to smoking tobacco — 22%

To help me reduce the amount of tobacco I smoke, but not stop completely — 22%

Because I had made an attempt to quit smoking already and I wanted an aid to help me keep off tobacco — 28%

To help me stop smoking tobacco entirely — 34%

Other — 19%

Base: 1,035 adults who had used e-cigarettes

FOR AND AGAINST

ASH (Action on Smoking and Health) estimates that there are **1.3 MILLION CURRENT USERS OF E-CIGARETTES IN THE UK.** These are almost all current or ex-smokers. Only a tiny number of non-smokers regularly use the product.

However the doctors' association, the BMA, is concerned that there has been no study of the effects of e-cigarettes. They are also concerned that because they look like ordinary cigarettes they will make smoking seem 'normal' again in public places. They want e-cigarettes to be included in the ban on smoking in public places.

Some issues

• Why do you think people continue to smoke, despite knowing the dangers?

• Would it help people give up smoking if they could use e-cigarettes in public places?

• What other reasons might there be for e-cigarette use to increase?

Drug deaths

The figures include accidents and suicides as well as deaths from drug abuse and drug dependence. Drug poisoning deaths include legal and illegal drugs, prescription and over the-counter medications as well as complications from drug abuse.

There were 2,597 drug poisoning deaths in 2012

Sources and weblinks:
Source: Deaths related to drug poisoning in England and Wales, 2012 © Crown copyright 2013
www.ons.gov.uk

Deaths among males decreased by 4% since 2011, to 1,706, the lowest number since 1995.

The equivalent number of female deaths rose to 891, an increase of 1% since 2011, and the highest since 2004.

The highest death rate from drug misuse was in 30 to 39-year-olds, at 97.8 deaths per million for men and 28.9 deaths per million for women in 2012.

Number of deaths from drug-related poisoning and drug misuse, by gender

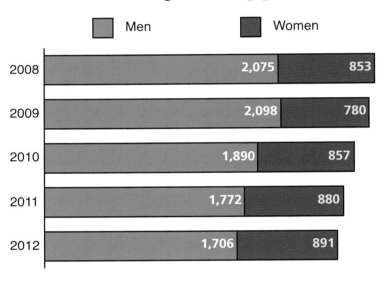

Legend: Men, Women

Year	Men	Women
2008	2,075	853
2009	2,098	780
2010	1,890	857
2011	1,772	880
2012	1,706	891

52% of all drug deaths involved an opiate drug, such as heroin. In fact in men aged 30 to 39 63% of these deaths involved an opiate.

Some issues

- Why do you think more men die from drug misuse than women?

- Who is responsible for reducing the number of drug deaths?

- If drugs were legal, would there be fewer deaths?

Body image

Cosmetic surgery

People are still keen to alter their bodies

There were **43,172** surgical procedures carried out in 2012.

Figures showed that although the number of cosmetic surgery procedures overall were similar to the previous year, anti-ageing treatments soared.

Sources and weblinks:
Source: British Association of Aesthetic Plastic Surgeons
www.baaps.org.uk

The top surgical procedures for men and women

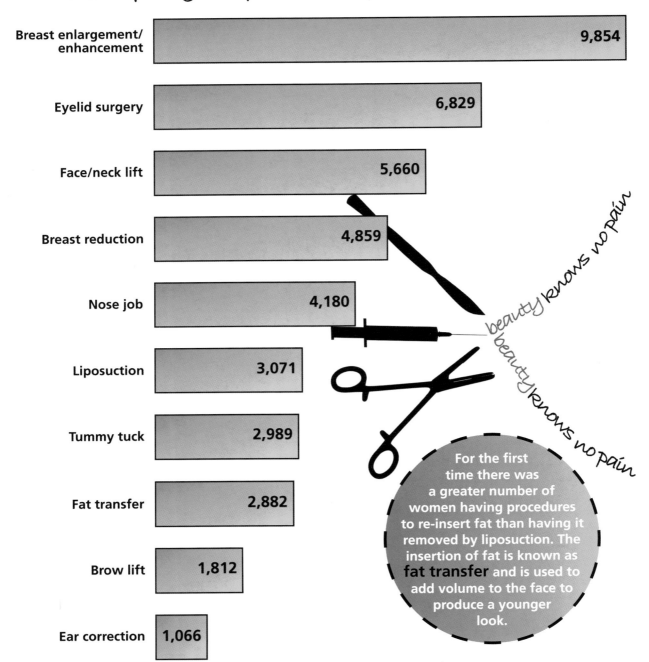

Procedure	Number
Breast enlargement/enhancement	9,854
Eyelid surgery	6,829
Face/neck lift	5,660
Breast reduction	4,859
Nose job	4,180
Liposuction	3,071
Tummy tuck	2,989
Fat transfer	2,882
Brow lift	1,812
Ear correction	1,066

beauty knows no pain
beauty knows no pain

For the first time there was a greater number of women having procedures to re-insert fat than having it removed by liposuction. The insertion of fat is known as **fat transfer** and is used to add volume to the face to produce a younger look.

Women had 39,070 procedures: 90.5% of all cosmetic procedures

Surgery (in order of popularity)	Number of procedures	% rise or fall from 2011
Breast enlargement/ enhancement	9,843	-1.6%
Eyelid surgery	6,071	+13%
Face/neck lift	5,324	+13.3%
Breast reduction	4,217	-6.3%
Nose job	3,228	-7%
Tummy tuck	2,882	-11%
Fat transfer	2,641	+13%
Liposuction	2,638	-14%
Brow lift	1,663	+17%
Ear correction	563	-13%

Men had 4,102 procedures: 9.5% of all cosmetic procedures

Surgery (in order of popularity)	Number of procedures	% rise or fall from 2011
Nose job	952	-9%
Eyelid surgery	758	+11%
Breast reduction	642	-18%
Ear correction	503	-3.5%
Liposuction	433	-15%
Face/neck lift	306	+14%
Fat transfer	241	+9.5
Brow lift	149	+19%
Tummy tuck	107	-14%
Breast enlargement/ enhancement	11	no change

Some issues

- Does it make sense to you that people decide to spend money on cosmetic surgery?

- Is it a good thing that people want to look younger?

- Do the benefits really outweigh the risks?

See also Body confidence page 20

Unhealthy feet

20% of UK women are embarrassed about their feet

The College of Podiatry surveyed 2,000 UK adults aged 18+ about their foot problems.

In a separate survey amongst podiatrists, they report that the biggest cause of foot problems in the UK is footwear, with a lack of public awareness of common foot complaints also contributing to the problem.

Sources and weblinks:
Source: The College of Podiatry
www.scpod.org

90% of women have suffered with a foot problem

Cover up

12% of women had resorted to covering up their feet in front of people or on a sunny day because they didn't like how their feet looked.

How many shoes?

When it comes to footwear, UK women have an average of **17 pairs of shoes** compared to just **8 pairs** for the average male.

The younger the woman, the higher the heel worn

20% of women aged 18-24 own a pair of six inch high heeled shoes compared to **10%** of those aged 25-42 and just **3%** of 35-44 year olds.

> " We all like to look good but it's important to take a common sense approach to footwear. High heels and flip flops are fine to wear occasionally but not all the time. For day to day wear you should opt for a well-fitting round toed shoe with a heel height of around 3cm. "
>
> **Lorraine Jones, The College of Podiatry**

Top foot problems suffered by women

1. Blisters (55%)
2. Cracked heels (45%)
3. Veruccas (28%)
4. Corns (24%)
5. Ingrown toe nails (20%) and Athletes foot (20%)
6. Bunions (13%)
7. Joint problems (11%)
8. Excessive foot odour (9%)
9. Arthritis (8.8%)
10. Muscular problems (8%)

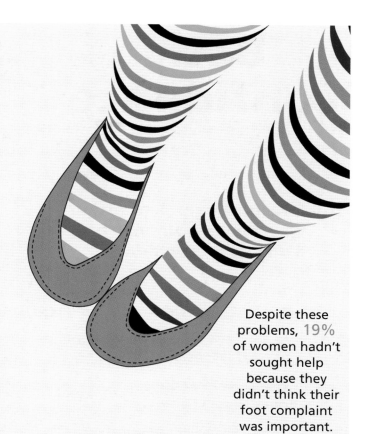

Despite these problems, 19% of women hadn't sought help because they didn't think their foot complaint was important.

Pain and discomfort

Women are also more likely than men to put up with discomfort and pain in the name of fashion.

43% of women admit they have continued to wear uncomfortable shoes even though they hurt their feet – twice as many as the men in the survey.

36% of women have worn shoes they knew didn't fit them because they looked nice; with just 12% of men reporting to have done the same.

Women report it takes an average of 1 hour, 6 minutes and 48 seconds for their feet to start hurting when they wear high heels.

20% say they start to feel pain within just 10 minutes.

37% say they have walked home with no shoes on after a night out because their feet hurt.

28% have danced barefoot while on a night out because of foot pain.

> " Feet are one of the hardest working parts of the body and in a lifetime you will walk in excess of 150,000 miles...
> Most of us will suffer with some sort of foot complaint at some point in our lives but we are seeing a lot of cases which could have been prevented – particularly amongst women. "

Lorraine Jones, The College of Podiatry

Some issues

- Why are women prepared to suffer foot pain and men are not?

- Why are younger women more likely to wear very high heels?

- What is the attraction of having many different pairs of shoes?

See also Essential Articles 2014, Why do women let fashion gurus bring them to heel?, p28

Body confidence

The pressure to look a certain way comes from many different directions

Celebrities, magazines, advertisers and the fashion and fitness industries often promote a body "ideal" which is either unrealistic or unattainable for over 95% of the population.

A survey of 1,569 adults and young people across the UK explored public attitudes surrounding body image-related issues.

Sources and weblinks:

Source: Central YMCA and Centre for Appearance Research, Body confidence campaign, Debenhams
www.ymca.co.uk
www1.uwe.ac.uk/hls/research/appearanceresearch
www.debenhams.com

What do the public think about...

...their bodies?

At least 25% of **adults** felt depressed about their bodies.

54.1% of the young girls surveyed said that girls at their school had body image problems and 23.7% thought that boys had body image problems.

...body diversity?

48.9% of adults said they wanted to see different body shapes and sizes, varieties of ages, ethnicities and a wider range of physical appearances in the media, advertising and fashion industries and on TV.

...models in magazines?

35.2% of **girls**; 30% of **women**; and 42.4% of **men** said they would like their bodies to look like the models who appear in magazines.

...people on TV?

25.4% of **girls**; 50.4% of **women**; and 36.8% of **men** said that they compared their bodies to people on TV.

...airbrushing?

Over half of the men surveyed were surprised by the extent of airbrushing in images presented to them.

Most men and women agreed that airbrushing had a negative impact on people's body image.

☐ Men   ☐ Women

80.9%

70.6%

Those who thought consumers were not aware of the extent to which images of people in the media have been airbrushed

Debenhams is promoting positive body image – the store has run trials with size 16 mannequins in windows, worked with disabled models and paralympians.

It also uses un-airbrushed lingerie photography – many retailers alter pictures of models to make them 'perfect'.

BEFORE: Un-retouched

" Fashion and beauty imagery that is honest, is absolutely crucial for all women to see...

The model is naturally gorgeous and doesn't need any retouching but the BEFORE and AFTER images show an example of just how much the image could have been altered, including all of the following:

- Face and neck slimmed
- Under-eyes smoothed and lightened
- Teeth whitened
- Eyes whitened
- Waist pulled in
- Arms slimmed
- Tidy hands
- Underarms tidied
- Legs made thinner
- Stray hairs tidied
- Skin tone changed, smoothed and brightened
- Cleavage enhanced "

Caryn Franklin, fashion commentator and co-founder of All Walks Beyond the Catwalk

AFTER: Retouched

Photos courtesy of Debenhams

The public were asked to what extent they would be prepared to adopt a quick fix solution to feel better about their bodies:

What do the public think about quick fixes?

☐ Men   ☐ Women

70.9% Women

44.5% Men

Those who had been on a diet in an attempt to change their body shape

- **8.5%** of men would consider taking *steroids* to change their body shape.

- **28.2%** of men and **31.4%** of women believed that *cosmetic surgery* was too readily available and should be restricted to those with underlying health issues – despite this, if money wasn't an issue **24%** of men and **29.5%** of women would have cosmetic surgery to change their body shape.

What do young people think about quick fixes?

- **34.4%** of boys and **49.1%** of girls had been on a diet in an attempt to change their body shape or to lose weight.

- **17.7%** of boys had taken protein supplements to make themselves more muscular.

- **11.1%** boys said they would take steroids to build muscle if they were unhappy with the way they looked.

- **8.3%** of boys and **7.7%** of girls would start taking laxatives to lose weight if they were unhappy with the way they looked.

- Nearly **15%** of girls would start taking diet pills to lose weight if they were unhappy with the way they looked.

- The most desired cosmetic procedures among young people were:
  - Breast implants – **14.7%**
  - Rhinoplasty (nose surgery) – **7.7%** of boys and **11.5%** of girls
  - Botox – **9.8%** of girls

Some issues

- Do you think that an 'ideal' body shape is promoted deliberately by advertisers and the fashion industry?

- Are the pressures greater on women than men or just different?

- Are quick fixes ok or are they risky?

See also Cosmetic surgery, p16 and Essential Articles 2014, One size doesn't fit all, p26

Britain & its citizens

Public perceptions

Research shows that what the public *thinks* is often very different from the *facts*

1,015 people in Great Britain aged 16 to 75 were questioned about ten key social issues.

Sources and weblinks:
Source: Ipsos MORI for the Royal Statistical Society and King's College London
www.ipsos-mori.com

Benefits savings

33% of the public think that capping benefits at £26,000 per household will save most money – in fact, it is estimated to save £290 million.

By comparison £5 billion would be saved by raising the pension age and £1.7 billion by stopping child benefit for wealthier households.

Teen pregnancy

The public think that 15% of girls under 16 get pregnant each year – this is **25 times higher** than official estimates of around 0.6%.

Benefit fraud

The public think that £24 out of every £100 spent on benefits is claimed fraudulently, **34 times more** than official estimates of £0.70 per £100.

Religion

On average the public think that 24% of the population are Muslims – the actual proportion is just 5% in England and Wales.

And, on average, the public think that 34% of the population are Christians – the actual proportion is 59% in England and Wales.

Foreign aid

26% of the public think that foreign aid is one of the top items the government spends most money on – in reality it actually makes up only 1.1% of expenditure (£7.9bn) in the 2011/12 financial year.

Immigration...

The public *think* that 31% of the population are immigrants – official figures are 13%. Even in estimates *including illegal immigrants* the figure is only about 15%.

...& ethnicity

The public *think* that Black and Asian people make up 30% of the population, when it is actually 11% (or 14% if mixed and other non-white ethnic groups are included).

Voting

The public *think* that, on average, the proportion of people who voted in the last general election is 43%, when 65% of the electorate actually did (51% of the whole population).

Age

The public's *average estimate is that 36% of the population are 65+*, when only 16% actually are.

Crime

58% do NOT believe that crime is falling – the Crime Survey for England and Wales actually shows that *incidents of crime were 19% lower* in 2012 than in 2006/07 and 53% lower than in 1995.

51% *think* that *violent crime is rising*, when it has *fallen from almost 2.5 million incidents* in 2006/07 to *under 2 million* in 2012.

Jobseeker's Allowance

29% of the public *think* that *we spend more on Jobseeker's Allowance than pensions*, when in fact *we spend 15 times more on pensions* (£4.9 billion on Jobseeker's Allowance compared to £74.2 billion on pensions).

Some issues

- Why do people have such a false idea about actual figures?

- Could schools teach people to interpret statistics more accurately?

- Why is knowing the facts about numbers important in each of the areas mentioned?

Progress on prejudice

Britain is a fairer and less racist country than it was 20 years ago

April 2013 was the 20th anniversary of the racially motivated murder of Stephen Lawrence in 1993.

A national poll of 2,032 adults showed how much general levels of prejudice in Britain have changed.

Sources and weblinks:
Source: The Integration Consensus 1993-2013: How Britain has changed since Stephen Lawrence, British Future
www.britishfuture.org

Do you think levels of racial prejudice in 1993 were...

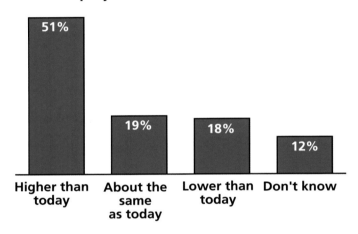

- **51%** Higher than today
- **19%** About the same as today
- **18%** Lower than today
- **12%** Don't know

Looking ahead to 2018...

- **24%** thought racial prejudice would be higher than today
- **44%** said about the same as today
- **20%** said lower than today
- **12%** didn't know

How much prejudice do you think there is against each of these ethnic groups?

NB Figures may not add up to 100% due to rounding

A lot   **A little**   **Hardly any**   **Don't know**

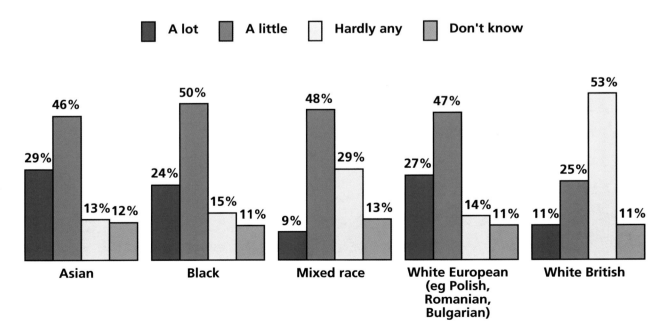

Asian: 29%, 46%, 13%, 12%
Black: 24%, 50%, 15%, 11%
Mixed race: 9%, 48%, 29%, 13%
White European (eg Polish, Romanian, Bulgarian): 27%, 47%, 14%, 11%
White British: 11%, 25%, 53%, 11%

There are a number of forms of prejudice that people of ethnic minorities can face. Do you think this happens more, less or the same as it did 20 years ago?

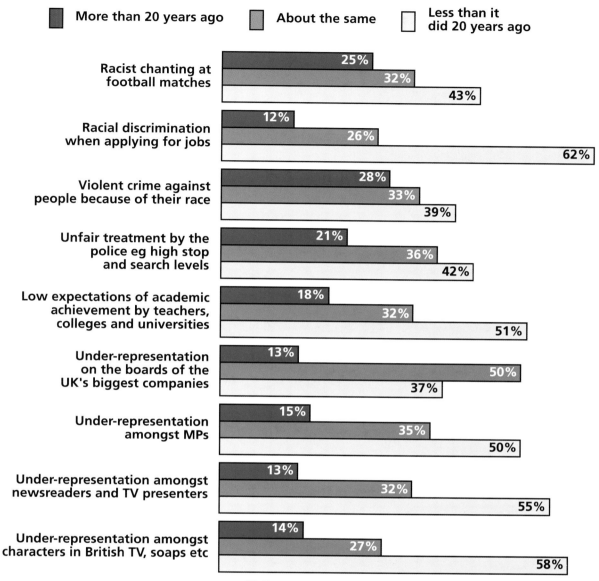

More than 20 years ago **About the same** **Less than it did 20 years ago**

Racist chanting at football matches
- 25%
- 32%
- 43%

Racial discrimination when applying for jobs
- 12%
- 26%
- 62%

Violent crime against people because of their race
- 28%
- 33%
- 39%

Unfair treatment by the police eg high stop and search levels
- 21%
- 36%
- 42%

Low expectations of academic achievement by teachers, colleges and universities
- 18%
- 32%
- 51%

Under-representation on the boards of the UK's biggest companies
- 13%
- 50%
- 37%

Under-representation amongst MPs
- 15%
- 35%
- 50%

Under-representation amongst newsreaders and TV presenters
- 13%
- 32%
- 55%

Under-representation amongst characters in British TV, soaps etc
- 14%
- 27%
- 58%

NB Figures may not add up to 100% due to rounding

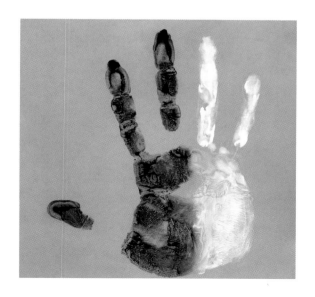

Some issues

- Most people feel that there is less racial prejudice today. Are they correct?

- Which of the forms of prejudice listed above is the most harmful?

- Two of the examples mention TV. How important is it in changing attitudes?

Mixed race population

Young people worry less about race than their parents did and see mixed race Britain as the everyday norm

The Census shows that Britain is becoming more ethnically diverse and the percentage of the population with a mixed heritage is increasing.

The think tank British Future commissioned research using a representative sample of 2,149 adults aged 18+ across Great Britain about their attitudes to racial mixing.

Sources and weblinks:
Source: The melting pot generation, British Future; Census 2011, Office for National Statistics © 2012
www.britishfuture.org
www.ons.gov.uk

Changing the nation

Jessica Ennis was the face of the Olympics. With her mixed race heritage she could stake a fair claim to being the face for the Census too.

In the 2001 census the mixed/ multiple ethnic group represented 1.4% of the population. By 2011 this group had risen to 2.2%.

Percentage make up of England & Wales, by ethnic group, 2011

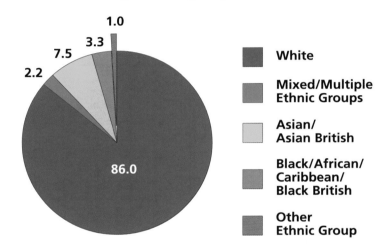

1.0
3.3
7.5
2.2
86.0

- White
- Mixed/Multiple Ethnic Groups
- Asian/ Asian British
- Black/African/ Caribbean/ Black British
- Other Ethnic Group

How comfortable are you with relationships between different races?

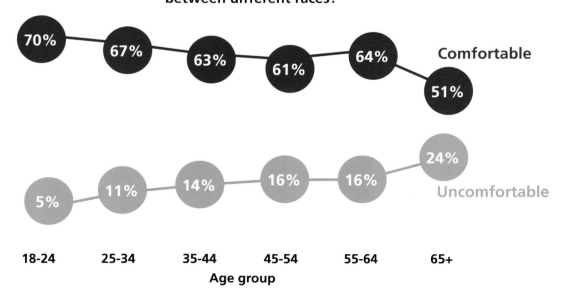

	18-24	25-34	35-44	45-54	55-64	65+
Comfortable	70%	67%	63%	61%	64%	51%
Uncomfortable	5%	11%	14%	16%	16%	24%

Age group

Would you be comfortable or uncomfortable if your children married someone who is/has...

(net*)

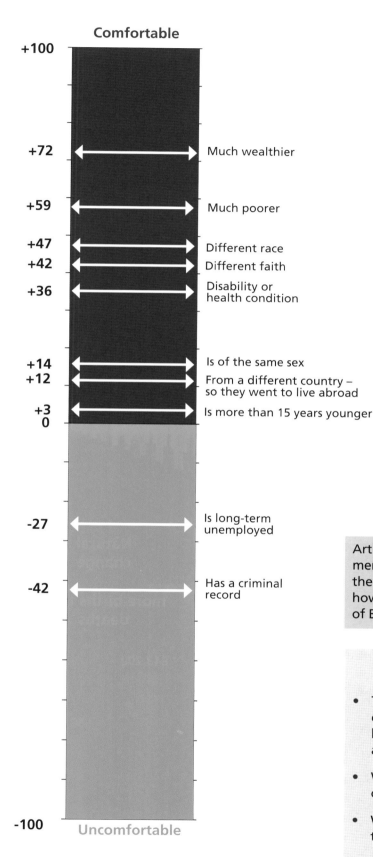

Comfortable

+100

+72 ← Much wealthier

+59 ← Much poorer

+47 ← Different race
+42 ← Different faith

+36 ← Disability or health condition

+14 ← Is of the same sex
+12 ← From a different country – so they went to live abroad

+3 ← Is more than 15 years younger
0

-27 ← Is long-term unemployed

-42 ← Has a criminal record

-100

Uncomfortable

*The net figure is calculated by finding the difference between the percentage who were comfortable and the percentage who were uncomfortable with each idea.

Articles involving Ennis saw 46 times as many mentions of "Sheffield" (her home town) as there were of "mixed race". This indicates how much racial mixture is an accepted part of Britain today.

Some issues

• The majority of people of all ages are comfortable with mixed race relationships but there is still a difference across the age groups. How would you explain this?

• Would your priorities be the same as the ones on the graph?

• What do these statistics suggest about the future of Britain?

See also Essential Articles 2014, Face of the future, p36

Increasing population

The population of the UK reached 63.7 million in 2012. Comparing this with 2011 and 2001 allows us to see the trend

The population of the UK grew by 0.7% between 2011 and 2012. This was accounted for by natural change (births and deaths) and by international migration.

Sources and weblinks:
Source: Annual mid-year population estimates, 2011 and 2012 Office for National Statistics
© Crown copyright 2013
www.ons.gov.uk

Population distribution of the United Kingdom 2012, by country (millions)

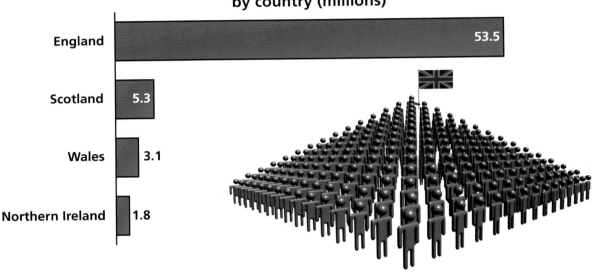

Country	Population
England	53.5
Scotland	5.3
Wales	3.1
Northern Ireland	1.8

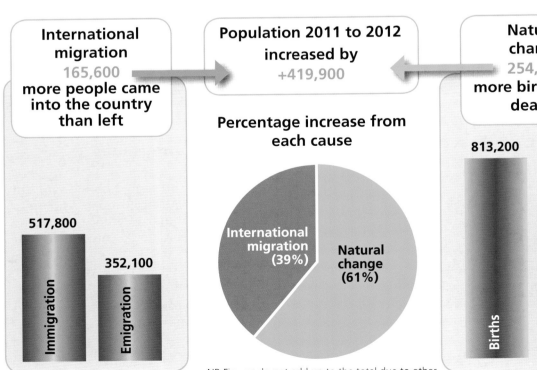

International migration
165,600
more people came into the country than left

Population 2011 to 2012 increased by
+419,900

Natural change
254,400
more births than deaths

Percentage increase from each cause

Immigration 517,800
Emigration 352,100

International migration (39%)
Natural change (61%)

Births 813,200
Deaths 558,800

NB Figures do not add up to the total due to other small changes accounting for a reduction of 100 people

Population in thousands, by age and gender, 2001 and 2012

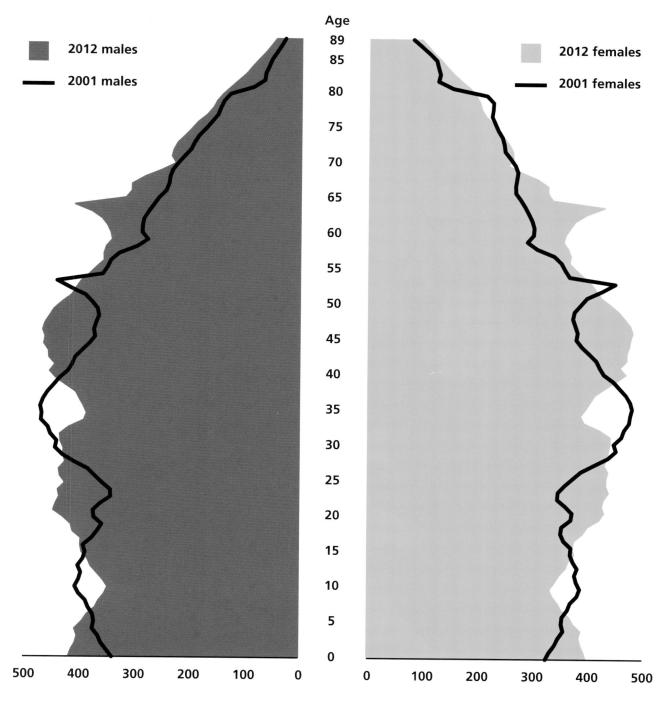

2012 males
2001 males

Age

2012 females
2001 females

500 400 300 200 100 0

0 100 200 300 400 500

The pyramid shows some important population trends

Immigration: For the most part the shape of the 2012 pyramid is similar to 2001 but shifted 11 years on as each part of the population moves up the age range. For example, the peaks in the black lines at age 50-55 show in the 2012 pyramid between 60 and 65.

Looking at the 23 to 33 age group, the 2012 pyramid shows a much wider and flatter shape than you would expect. This can only be caused by new population being added from outside the UK.

Fewer deaths: The number of males aged 75 and over in the UK has increased by **26%** since 2001, compared to an increase of slightly more than **6%** for females. This is largely because of changes in smoking habits, advances in treating circulatory illnesses and because many 'male' jobs have become less physical and safer.

More births: There are **581,800** more zero to six year olds in 2012 than there were in 2001.

Change in population, by country and region, 2001 to 2012

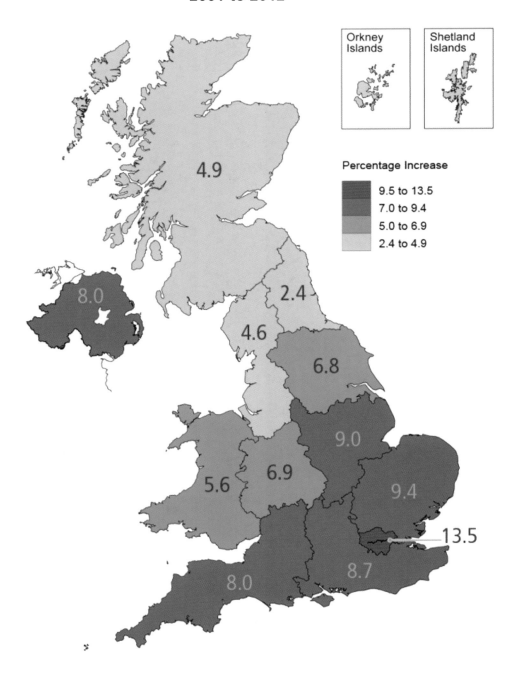

Orkney Islands

Shetland Islands

Percentage Increase

- 9.5 to 13.5
- 7.0 to 9.4
- 5.0 to 6.9
- 2.4 to 4.9

4.9

8.0

2.4

4.6

6.8

9.0

5.6

6.9

9.4

13.5

8.0

8.7

The population of the UK as a whole increased by **7.8%** in the 11 years between 2001 and 2012, with the greatest increase in London and the south of England.

These areas also showed the highest growth between 2011 and 2012.

London had the highest natural growth rate, with **86,000** more births than deaths. It was also the destination of a third of all international migrants arriving in the UK.

Some issues

- How much population growth is a good thing?

- Why is the population increase different in different parts of the country?

- Two elements which have added most to population growth are more births and people living longer. What benefits and what problems might this natural increase bring?

Ethnic population

England and Wales have become more ethnically diverse

The White ethnic group accounted for **86%** of the usual resident population in 2011, a decrease from **91.3%** in 2001.

Despite this decrease, it is still the majority ethnic group.

Sources and weblinks:
Source: 2011 Census, Office for National Statistics © Crown copyright 2012
www.ons.gov.uk

Population by ethnic groups, England and Wales (thousands) ■ 2001 ■ 2011

Ethnic category questionnaire changes mean that:
* comparability issues exist between these groups
** no comparable data exists for these groups

White

Irish	642
	531
Gypsy or Irish Traveller**	58
Other White	46,879
	47,621

Mixed/ multiple ethnic groups

White and Black Caribbean	237
	427
White and Asian	189
	342
White and Black African	79
	166
Other Mixed	156
	290

Asian/ Asian British

Indian	1,037
	1,413
Pakistani	715
	1,125
Bangladeshi	281
	447
Chinese*	227
	393
Other Asian*	241
	836

Black/African/ Caribbean/ Black British

African	480
	990
Caribbean	564
	595
Other Black	96
	280

Other ethnic group

Arab**	231
Any other ethnic group*	220
	333

London was the most ethnically diverse area and Wales the least.

Some issues

• What factors might affect the number of different ethnic groups in a country?

• Do the numbers on this graph reflect the people you see around you and the people that you know?

• Why might the census questions change from one decade to the next?

Faith symbols

There is overwhelming public support for the freedom to wear small religious items at work... but not for the burka

Nadia Eweida was sent home from work by British Airways in 2006, for breaching uniform code after she refused to remove a necklace with a Christian cross. She took her case to the European Court of Human Rights (ECHR) and in January 2013 she was paid £1,600 in damages and £25,000 in costs.

In January 2013, two surveys with over 1,900 British adults aged 18+ in each, revealed attitudes to wearing religious items at work.

Sources and weblinks:
Source: YouGov-Cambridge
http://cambridge.yougov.com

Do you think people in the UK SHOULD or SHOULD NOT be allowed to wear a necklace with a Christian cross while working in the following roles?

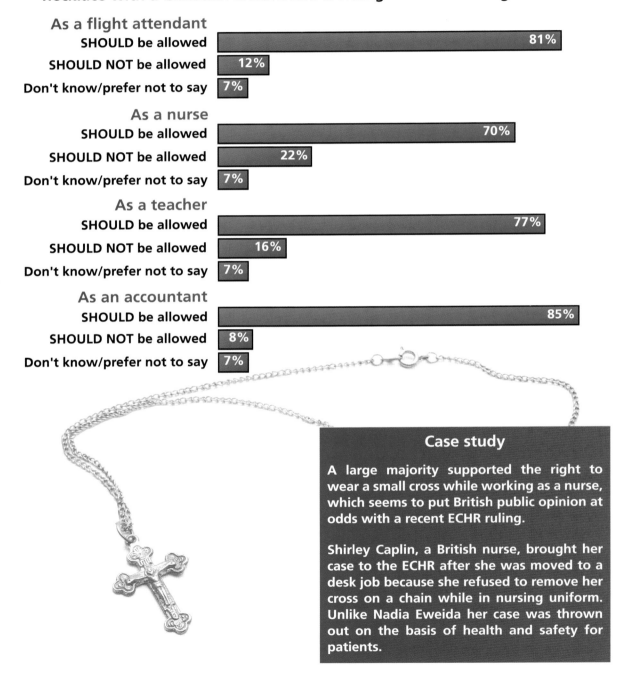

As a flight attendant
- SHOULD be allowed — 81%
- SHOULD NOT be allowed — 12%
- Don't know/prefer not to say — 7%

As a nurse
- SHOULD be allowed — 70%
- SHOULD NOT be allowed — 22%
- Don't know/prefer not to say — 7%

As a teacher
- SHOULD be allowed — 77%
- SHOULD NOT be allowed — 16%
- Don't know/prefer not to say — 7%

As an accountant
- SHOULD be allowed — 85%
- SHOULD NOT be allowed — 8%
- Don't know/prefer not to say — 7%

Case study

A large majority supported the right to wear a small cross while working as a nurse, which seems to put British public opinion at odds with a recent ECHR ruling.

Shirley Caplin, a British nurse, brought her case to the ECHR after she was moved to a desk job because she refused to remove her cross on a chain while in nursing uniform. Unlike Nadia Eweida her case was thrown out on the basis of health and safety for patients.

Do you think people in the UK SHOULD or SHOULD NOT be allowed to wear a burka while working in the following roles?

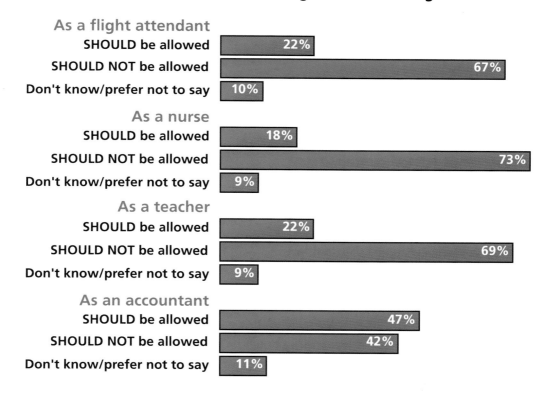

As a flight attendant

SHOULD be allowed	22%
SHOULD NOT be allowed	67%
Don't know/prefer not to say	10%

As a nurse

SHOULD be allowed	18%
SHOULD NOT be allowed	73%
Don't know/prefer not to say	9%

As a teacher

SHOULD be allowed	22%
SHOULD NOT be allowed	69%
Don't know/prefer not to say	9%

As an accountant

SHOULD be allowed	47%
SHOULD NOT be allowed	42%
Don't know/prefer not to say	11%

Attitudes to the burka

There are clear limits to British support for religious clothing at work when it comes to the burka.

Part of this opposition could relate to practical issues regarding the burka. People might presume rightly or wrongly that the burka has a greater impact on certain activities than a small cross on a chain.

In other surveys, there has been a constant majority of over two thirds who support banning the burka in the UK as they have done in France.

This would mean not only barring it from the workplace but making it illegal even to wear one while walking down the street.

The UK Minister of State for Police and Criminal Justice said that such a ban in the UK would be 'un-British' and against the UK's 'tolerant and mutually respectful society'.

Some issues

- Why do you think there is opposition to the burka?

- Would the size or style of the religious symbol have any influence on whether it was appropriate?

- Setting aside religion, who should decide on a correct dress code for work?

See also Essential Articles 13, Why the burka is part of Britain, p26 and They are right to ban the burka, p29

Childhood freedom

Children in England have far less freedom to move about their neighbourhoods than they used to have

Researchers from the Policy Studies Institute gave questionnaires to children and their parents in five locations in England and five in Germany in 1971, 1990 and 2010.

Each questionnaire gave a 'snapshot' of the children's ability to move around independently.

Sources and weblinks:
Source: Children's Independent Mobility in England and Germany, 1971-2010,
© *Policy Studies Institute 2012*
www.psi.org.uk

Percentage of children in England allowed to travel home from Primary school alone

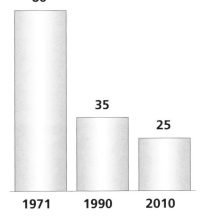

1971	1990	2010
86	35	25

Percentage of children in England allowed to travel without an adult to weekend activities

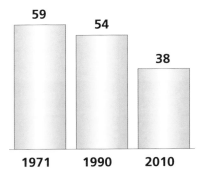

1971	1990	2010
59	54	38

Percentage of primary school children in 2010 who said they were allowed to:

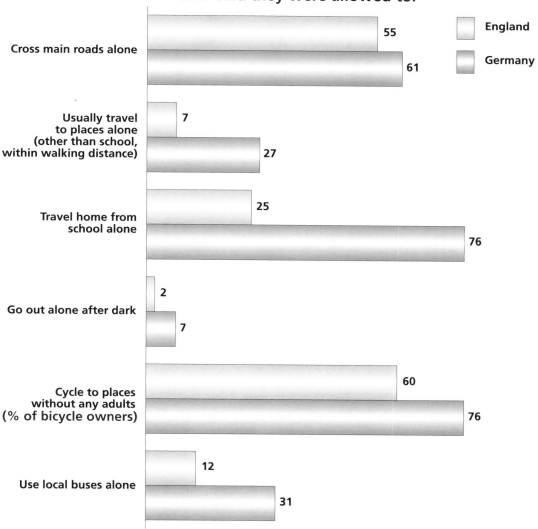

England | **Germany**

	England	Germany
Cross main roads alone	55	61
Usually travel to places alone (other than school, within walking distance)	7	27
Travel home from school alone	25	76
Go out alone after dark	2	7
Cycle to places without any adults (% of bicycle owners)	60	76
Use local buses alone	12	31

Some issues

- At what age do you think children should be allowed to do each thing mentioned in the graph?

- What reasons can you suggest for the change in the amount of freedom children have now compared to 1971?

- Why do these freedoms matter?

See also Essential Articles 2014, Why don't we encourage young people to grow up? p204 and Grown up at 12? p206

Trends in home ownership

Over the last century, the pattern of home ownership has changed

There has been a rapid increase in private renters which can be linked to the difficulties of getting on the housing ladder.

The last decade has seen the first rise in the percentage of households renting, since 1918.

Sources and weblinks:
*Source: A Century of Home Ownership and Renting in England and Wales – Office for National Statistics © Crown copyright 2013
www.ons.gov.uk*

A century of home ownership and renting

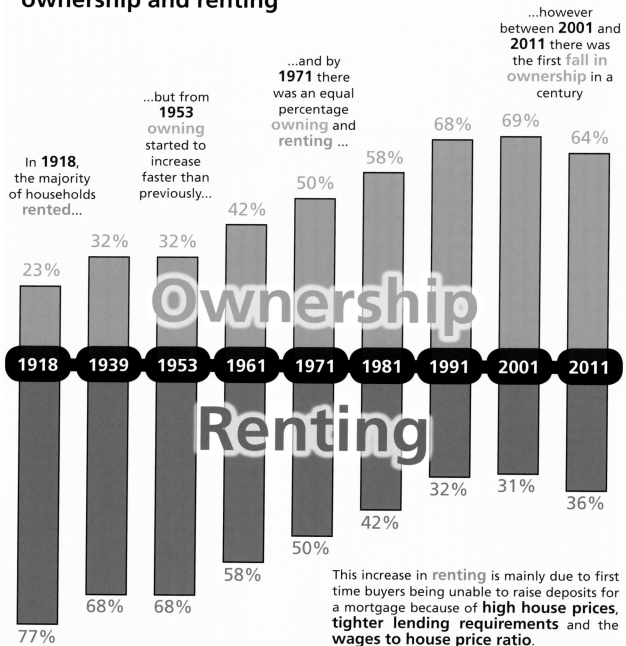

In **1918**, the majority of households rented...

...but from **1953** owning started to increase faster than previously...

...and by **1971** there was an equal percentage owning and renting ...

...however between **2001** and **2011** there was the first fall in ownership in a century

Ownership

| 1918 | 1939 | 1953 | 1961 | 1971 | 1981 | 1991 | 2001 | 2011 |

Ownership: 23% | 32% | 32% | 42% | 50% | 58% | 68% | 69% | 64%

Renting

Renting: 77% | 68% | 68% | 58% | 50% | 42% | 32% | 31% | 36%

This increase in renting is mainly due to first time buyers being unable to raise deposits for a mortgage because of **high house prices, tighter lending requirements** and the **wages to house price ratio**.

Home ownership and renting – 2001 and 2011 comparison

2001

21.7m
households
in England and
Wales...

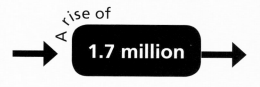

A rise of
1.7 million

2011

23.4m
households
in England and
Wales...

14.9m
were **owner occupiers**

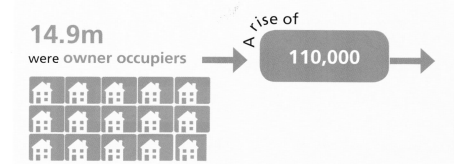

A rise of
110,000

15.0m
were **owner occupiers**

6.7m
rented their homes

A rise of
1.6 million

8.3m
rented their homes

London had the highest percentage of **renters**, accounting for **50.4%** of households in the region. This is about 15 percentage points higher than the average for England and Wales.

Some issues

- Is owning your own home an important aim in life?

- Whose responsibility is it to make sure that everyone has good, affordable housing?

- Why is London so different from the other regions?

- Why is it more difficult to get on the housing ladder now?

See also Essential Articles 2014, If every man or woman's home is their castle, who cares if it costs £1 to buy? p86

Politeness in Britain

The majority of Britons think we're quick to thank and apologise – but slow to open doors and give up our seats

A survey of 1,903 people revealed how British adults regard the manners of fellow citizens.

Sources and weblinks:
Source: YouGov
www.yougov.co.uk

Which groups are the LEAST polite?

24% say the upper class are least polite, **14%** say working class people are and **39%** think teenagers are rudest.

Which groups are the MOST polite?

21% say the middle classes are most courteous and **29%** say those in their fifties and sixties are most polite.

How many people do you think WOULD...

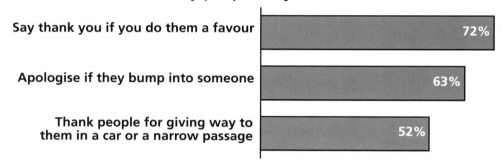

Say thank you if you do them a favour	72%
Apologise if they bump into someone	63%
Thank people for giving way to them in a car or a narrow passage	52%

How many people do you think WOULDN'T...

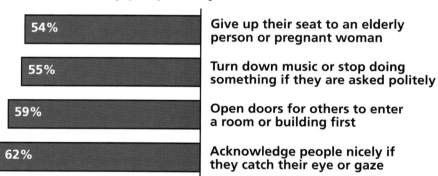

54%	Give up their seat to an elderly person or pregnant woman
55%	Turn down music or stop doing something if they are asked politely
59%	Open doors for others to enter a room or building first
62%	Acknowledge people nicely if they catch their eye or gaze

THANK YOU!

Some issues

- Does politeness matter?
- Is it fair to say teenagers are the rudest group?
- Are you more or less polite depending on circumstances?

See also Essential Articles 2014, International Day of Happiness: Ways to turn that frown upside-down, p122

Care &
carers

Assisted dying

70% of GB adults support a change in the law to permit assisted dying

Euthanasia is the act of deliberately ending a person's life to relieve suffering.

Assisted suicide is the act of deliberately assisting or encouraging another person to commit, or attempt to commit, suicide.

A poll of 4,437 GB adults revealed the reasons people have for supporting or opposing a change in the law.

Sources and weblinks:
*Source: YouGov poll for Westminster Faith Debate
– Religion & Society, Lancaster University; BBC
www.religionandsociety.org.uk
www.bbc.co.uk*

Euthanasia and assisted suicide are illegal in the UK.

Currently, anyone who aids the suicide of another person can be put in prison for up to 14 years. A change in the law would remove the risk of prosecution.

Other countries, like Switzerland, do permit it in specific circumstances. Dignitas is the only Swiss clinic which will accept foreigners who wish to end their lives.

All those who thought the current law on euthanasia should be changed to allow assisted suicide in some circumstances were asked which of the following best described their view

(more than one answer could be given)

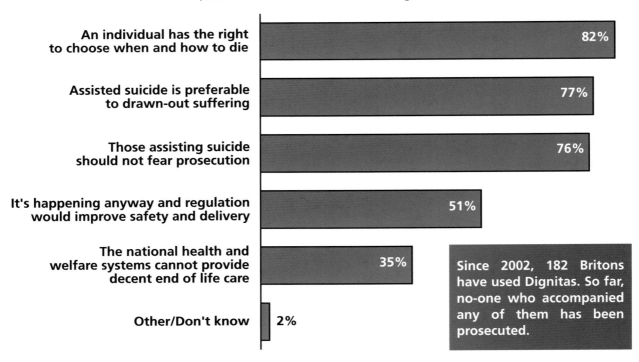

View	%
An individual has the right to choose when and how to die	82%
Assisted suicide is preferable to drawn-out suffering	77%
Those assisting suicide should not fear prosecution	76%
It's happening anyway and regulation would improve safety and delivery	51%
The national health and welfare systems cannot provide decent end of life care	35%
Other/Don't know	2%

Since 2002, 182 Britons have used Dignitas. So far, no-one who accompanied any of them has been prosecuted.

Religion

81% of those who said they had no religion **supported a change in the law.**

64% of religious people **supported a change in the law.**

All those who thought the current law on euthanasia should be kept as it is were asked which of the following best described their view

(more than one answer could be given)

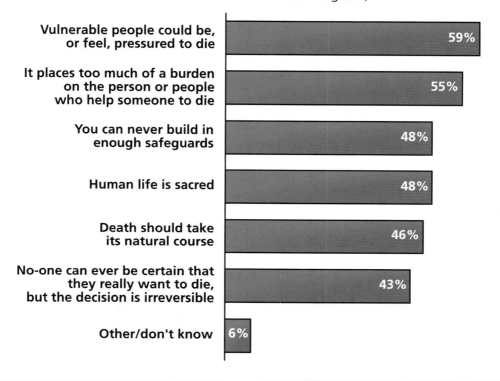

View	%
Vulnerable people could be, or feel, pressured to die	59%
It places too much of a burden on the person or people who help someone to die	55%
You can never build in enough safeguards	48%
Human life is sacred	48%
Death should take its natural course	46%
No-one can ever be certain that they really want to die, but the decision is irreversible	43%
Other/don't know	6%

Professor Linda Woodhead, professor of sociology of religion at Lancaster University, said modern medical advances had changed people's attitudes about death.

"We are used to having more control over our lives and I think that is partly why there is this overwhelming number of people saying that they have a right to decide for themselves."

Some issues

- Who should be involved in making a decision about when to die?

- How could you protect vulnerable people?

- Do you think a change in the law would make us a better society or a worse one?

Dying wishes

The majority of people in Britain have not discussed or made any plans for when they die...

... as a result, they are risking not getting appropriate end of life care and making it harder for their families to deal with bereavement.

2,145 adults in Britain were interviewed in 2012 about their attitudes to dying.

Sources and weblinks:
Source: NatCen Social Research
www.natcen.ac.uk

What do people want?

Q: If you were terminally ill, would you like to be told, or would you prefer not to know?

85% of respondents stated that they **would** like to be told.

79% of those **aged 75+** years **wouldn't** want to be told.

Q: When the time comes, where do you think would be the best place to die?

67% said that they would prefer to die at home.

Despite the overwhelming preference for dying at home, only **12%** had ever discussed with anyone their preferred place to die.

Discussing death

People are generally confident about discussing death and planning for the end of life...

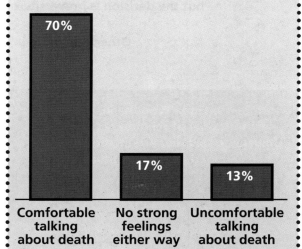

Comfortable talking about death	No strong feelings either way	Uncomfortable talking about death
70%	17%	13%

...yet this comfort and confidence is not always translated into actual discussion and practical planning

What's stopping people from talking about dying?

43% of all age groups **hadn't** discussed their wishes largely because death was seen as far off.

The main reason given by people in the 75+ age group was that other people did not want to talk to them about their death. **28%** said this.

What would make people discuss dying?

To make it easier for family or friends was the main reason for **63%** of respondents.

To ensure the right care and support for themselves when they were dying was the main reason for a minority, **15%**.

Planning

76% of respondents stated that they **did not** have any written plans about their wishes in relation to dying.

Overall **12%** of respondents stated that they had written wishes about **organ donations**.

Finances

73% of respondents said they felt confident that they could make adequate financial plans for the end of life, but only **3%** of this group actually had a plan for how they would support themselves financially.

Funeral

Similarly, even among those stating that they are confident about being able to plan their own funerals, only **13%** actually had a written document containing their funeral wishes/plan.

Despite the reluctance to discuss the matter openly – and the relatively low numbers having actually made any provision in practical terms – **79%** stated that they felt confident about planning for the right sort of care and support at the end of life.

"You don't have to be ill or dying to make plans for your future."

Eve Richardson, Chief Executive of the Dying Matters Coalition and the National Council for Palliative Care

Some issues

• Why is it so difficult to make a definite plan for the end of life?

• Would you like to plan the details of your own funeral?

• Do you think that knowing that someone near to you had an end of life plan would make you feel happy or would it be sad?

See also Essential Articles 2014, I need my mother by my side, how can I stand by and watch her die? p118

Quality of care

People feel more cared for when health staff are polite and understanding

Around 64,500 NHS patients aged 16+ were surveyed about their experiences of the care and treatment they received in hospital.

80% of respondents overall said they were always treated with respect and dignity while in hospital but there were still concerns and room for improvement in other areas.

Sources and weblinks:
Source: National NHS patient survey programme; Care Quality Commission
www.cqc.org.uk

Communication with doctors

Q When you had important questions to ask a doctor, did you get answers that you could understand?

68% said yes, always. 26% said yes, sometimes.

Q Did you have confidence and trust in the doctors treating you?

80% said yes, always. 17% said yes, sometimes.

Q Did doctors talk in front of you as if you weren't there?

75% said no.

Care & privacy

Q Did you find someone on the hospital staff to talk to about your worries and fears?

38% said yes, definitely. 38% said yes, to some extent.

Q Do you feel you got enough emotional support from hospital staff during your stay?

56% said yes, always. 30% said yes, sometimes.

Q Were you given enough privacy when discussing your condition or treatment?

74% said yes, always. 19% said yes, sometimes.

Respect & dignity

"Everyone from the doctors downwards were extremely considerate and kind. I had excellent care from the nurses and always felt I was being treated as a human being not just a patient."

"I cannot fault any aspect of my treatment and care. I had a complete sense of well being throughout and was very impressed with all the services."

Room for improvement

"Majority of nurses extremely efficient and kind just a couple spoilt this by being quite uncaring and making the patient feel she was being a nuisance."

"The main problem with the hospital is lack of staff on the wards... the nurses/doctors do a fantastic job... under pressure they can't look after all the patients with the limited staff they have."

Some patients felt that they were **left alone**, were being **ignored** or **felt forgotten** and that staff were **not spending time** with patients:

"I would have liked to see my consultant as I have never met him or had a chance to discuss anything with him."

Another negative issue was the **hospital food** which was widely described as of **low quality and tasteless** – **30%** of people thought it was **fair** but **13%** described it as **poor**.

Most people responded positively though when asked to rate their overall experience

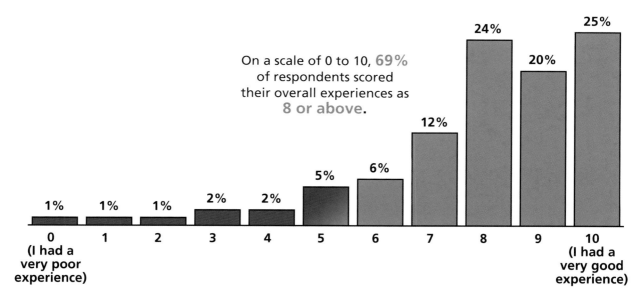

On a scale of 0 to 10, 69% of respondents scored their overall experiences as 8 or above.

0 (I had a very poor experience)	1	2	3	4	5	6	7	8	9	10 (I had a very good experience)
1%	1%	1%	2%	2%	5%	6%	12%	24%	20%	25%

Some issues

- What do you think matters most in giving patients a positive experience of hospital?

- Should 'how to be caring' be part of medical training?

- There is a suggestion that patients should pay for their food while in hospital. Is this a good idea?

See also Essential Articles 2014, The NHS prioritising those with a 'healthy lifestyle', p120

Young carers

166,363 children in England are caring for their parents, siblings and family members

The term **young carer** refers to children and young people under 18 who provide regular or ongoing care and emotional support to a family member who is physically or mentally ill, disabled or misuses substances.

The figures here use the latest census data from 2011 and a survey that tracked the lives of around 15,000 young people aged 13 and 14 over a seven-year period.

Sources and weblinks:

Source: Hidden from view: The experiences of young carers in England © The Children's Society, 2013
www.childrenssociety.org.uk/young-carers

The demands of caring can have an impact on carers' emotional or physical well-being or educational achievement and life chances.

How old are young carers?

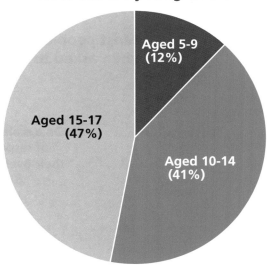

Aged 5-9 (12%)

Aged 15-17 (47%)

Aged 10-14 (41%)

Many young carers remain hidden from official sight for many reasons, including family loyalty, stigma, bullying and not knowing where to go for support.

Profile of a young carer

Young carers are 1.5 times more likely than their peers to have a special educational need or a disability.

They are 1.5 times more likely than their peers to be from black, Asian or minority ethnic communities, and are twice as likely not to speak English as their first language.

They are equally likely to be a girl or a boy.

There has been an overall increase in young carers over the last decade.

The sharpest rise was in the number of children under age 10 who were carers – there were more than 20,700 in England.

The number of 5 to 7 year old young carers has increased by around 80% to 9,371.

One in 12 young carers spends **more than 15 hours** a week caring

Who do young carers look after?

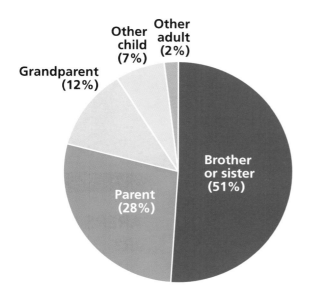

Other child (7%)
Other adult (2%)
Grandparent (12%)
Brother or sister (51%)
Parent (28%)

Education and prospects

Around **one in 20** young carers **misses school** because of their caring responsibilities.

They are gaining **fewer qualifications** and are therefore less likely to earn a decent living.

They have significantly **lower** educational attainment at **GCSE** level.

Young carers are **more likely** than the national average to be **not in education, employment or training** (NEET) between the ages of 16 and 19.

Missing out

Caring can prevent young people participating in all aspects of life.

They can miss out on a huge range of opportunities that others take for granted, from educational opportunities, to spending time with friends and having time and space to do their homework.

Some issues

- What reasons could there be for a young person to become a carer?

- Do you think there is any way that young people can be protected from taking on too much responsibility?

- Many young carers have difficult lives yet say they do not resent giving care to a family member. Is there any way they can be compensated for the opportunities they have lost?

Prepared to care

The big picture of caring in the UK today

2,115 carers from across the UK were surveyed to ask about their experiences and how caring impacted on their lives.

_____

Sources and weblinks:
Source: Prepared to Care? Exploring the impact of caring on people's lives, Carers Week © Carers UK 2013; NHS
www.carersuk.org
www.carersweek.org
www.nhs.uk

CARERS ACROSS THE UK:

NORTHERN IRELAND 214,000

SCOTLAND 516,000

WALES 370,000

ENGLAND 5,430,000

CARERS SAVE THE UK ECONOMY £119 BILLION EVERY YEAR

£119bn

EVERY DAY ANOTHER 6,000 PEOPLE TAKE ON A CARING RESPONSIBILITY

(That's over 2 million people a year)

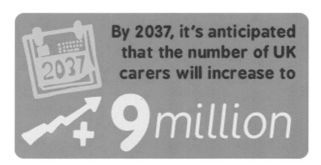

By 2037, it's anticipated that the number of UK carers will increase to **9 million**

WHO DO CARERS CARE FOR?

Parents/parents in law	40%
Spouse/partner	26%
Disabled children	8%
Adult children	5%
Grandparents	4%
Other relative	7%
Friend or neighbour	9%

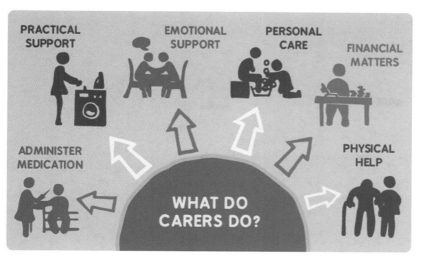

PRACTICAL SUPPORT

EMOTIONAL SUPPORT

PERSONAL CARE

FINANCIAL MATTERS

ADMINISTER MEDICATION

PHYSICAL HELP

WHAT DO CARERS DO?

Caring has an impact on **relationships, careers, finances** and a person's **health and well-being** both positively and negatively.

When someone becomes a carer it can happen suddenly or build gradually over time and many people do not recognise the effect it is having on their life.

Impact of caring on lives

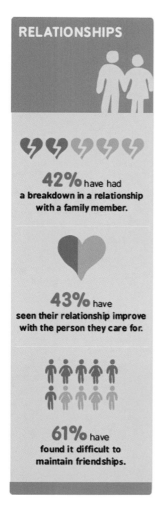

RELATIONSHIPS

42% have had a breakdown in a relationship with a family member.

43% have seen their relationship improve with the person they care for.

61% have found it difficult to maintain friendships.

CAREER

34% have missed out on the chance of promotion.

45% have given up work because of their caring role.

42% have reduced working hours because of a caring role.

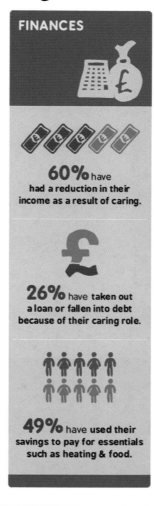

FINANCES

60% have had a reduction in their income as a result of caring.

26% have taken out a loan or fallen into debt because of their caring role.

49% have used their savings to pay for essentials such as heating & food.

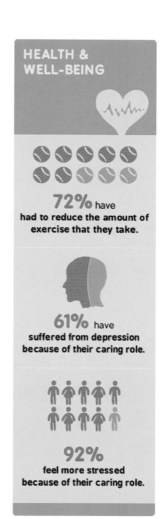

HEALTH & WELL-BEING

72% have had to reduce the amount of exercise that they take.

61% have suffered from depression because of their caring role.

92% feel more stressed because of their caring role.

75% of carers were **not prepared** for all aspects of caring.

81% were **not prepared** for the emotional impact of caring.

78% were **not prepared** for changes to their lifestyle because of a caring role.

71% were **not prepared** for the change in relationship with the person they care for.

63% of carers were **not prepared** for the impact caring had on their career.

72% were **not prepared** for the financial impact of their caring role.

Carers also mentioned how they struggled to readjust when their caring role ended or changed – especially if they had put their careers on hold, lost touch with friends or seen their personal finances reduced.

THREE IN FIVE
OF US WILL BE A CARER AT SOME POINT IN OUR LIVES

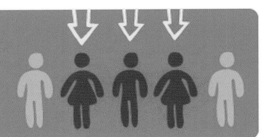

Support, advice and information

81% of carers were not aware of the support available and **35%** were given the wrong advice about support available because of the time it took them to identify themselves as carers.

Most carers have a legal right to an assessment of their own needs. **46%** of carers surveyed had been offered this Carer's Assessment which gives them a chance to discuss the help they need to balance caring with other aspects of their life, such as work and family.

6.5 MILLION PEOPLE
ARE UNPAID CARERS IN THE UK
(That's 1 in every 8 adults)

More than one in five people aged 50–59 provide some unpaid care

(1.5 million across the UK)

Carers' Advice line:
0808 808 7777

Some issues

- Is caring just something you do for the people you love? Or is it something society should contribute to?

- Why are there more people in the 50-59 age group who are carers?

- Why would it take some people time to "identify themselves as carers"?

- What sort of support do you think carers need?

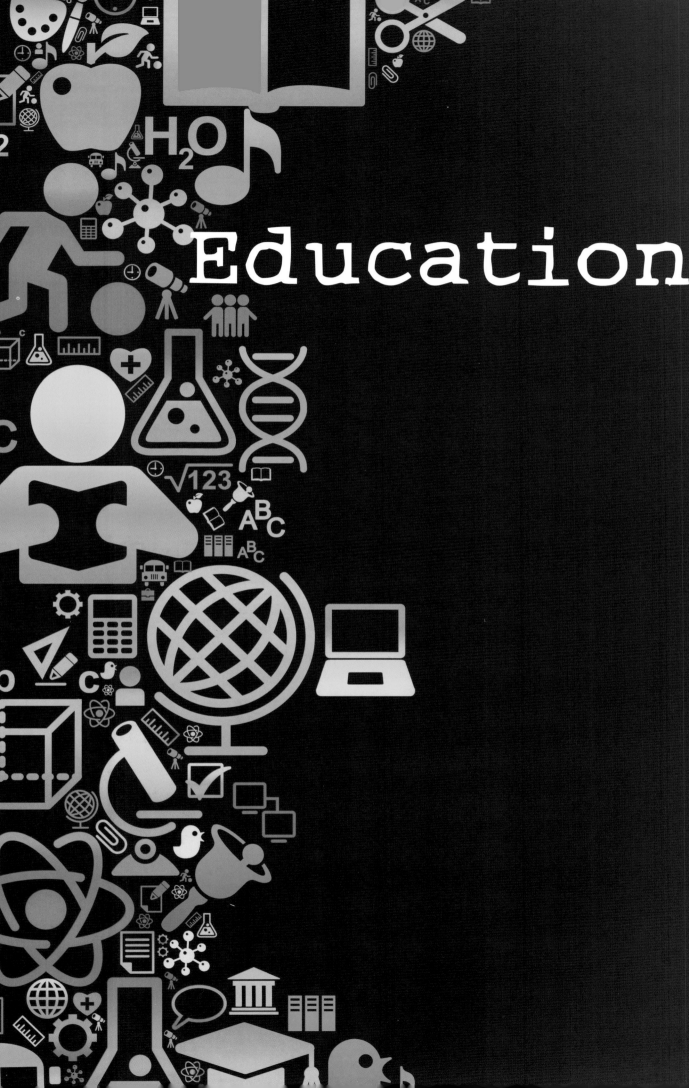

Education

Cost of school equipment

What children take to school and their school uniform may be costing too much

Retailer John Lewis worked out the top ten items taken to school and how much they cost. The Office of Fair Trading investigated the practice of schools specifying where uniforms can be bought.

Sources and weblinks:
Source: Bag to the future, John Lewis Ltd;
Supply of school uniforms, The Office of Fair Trading
© Crown copyright 2012
www.johnlewispresscentre.com
www.oft.gov.uk

According to the John Lewis chain of shops, the total cost of the contents of a school bag and school uniform in today's money:

in the *1960s* was *£231.20*

in the *1980s* was *£252.40*

The *total* cost in *2013* was *£550.80*.

This is because many school bags contain a *smart phone*, which costs around *£362.10*

Percentage of school bags containing these items: Top ten items and what they cost

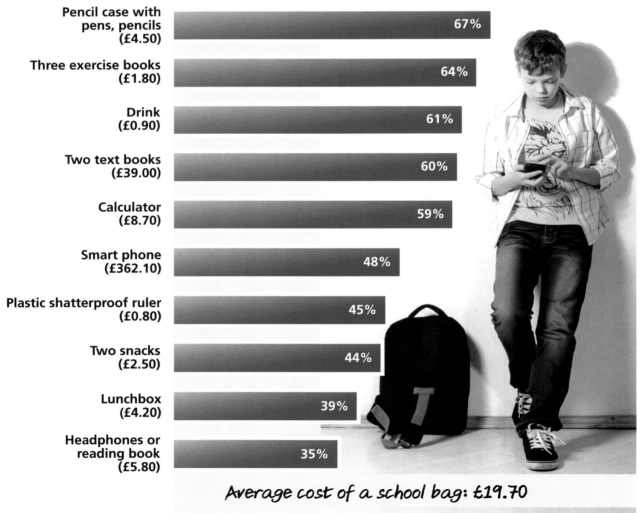

Item	Percentage
Pencil case with pens, pencils (£4.50)	67%
Three exercise books (£1.80)	64%
Drink (£0.90)	61%
Two text books (£39.00)	60%
Calculator (£8.70)	59%
Smart phone (£362.10)	48%
Plastic shatterproof ruler (£0.80)	45%
Two snacks (£2.50)	44%
Lunchbox (£4.20)	39%
Headphones or reading book (£5.80)	35%

Average cost of a school bag: £19.70

School uniform

79% of UK state schools insist that their pupils must wear a uniform of some kind, even if it is only one item.

Percentage of schools with a uniform, in which each item is compulsory

NB: items which are compulsory in more than 20% of schools. Some items are interchangeable eg skirts or trousers for girls.

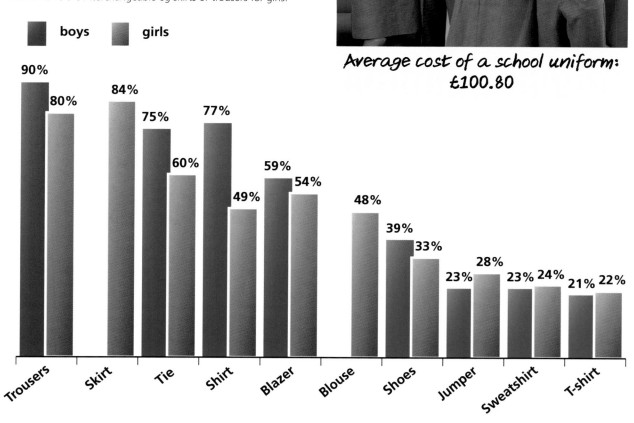

- boys
- girls

	boys	girls
Trousers	90%	80%
Skirt	84%	
Tie	75%	60%
Shirt	77%	49%
Blazer	59%	54%
Blouse		48%
Shoes	39%	33%
Jumper	23%	28%
Sweatshirt	23%	24%
T-shirt	21%	22%

Average cost of a school uniform: £100.80

Does restricting the suppliers mean parents have to spend more?

74% of the schools with uniform say that at least one item must be bought from selected shops or from the school itself.

The usual reason, given in **85%** of cases, was to make sure the uniform stayed consistent.

However, restricting the choice of shop can lead to large differences in price: for example a *boy's sweatshirt* from a specified shop cost on average **£12** and a *girl's skirt* averaged **£15.40**. This compares with **£5** each from a supermarket.

Some issues

- Is a smart phone an essential school item?

- Why do you think the majority of schools insist on a uniform?

- If you have a uniform, should all the items be identical or should there be room for difference?

- In Russia, rather than a school uniform, the government has said that all students and teachers must be dressed in just three colours: black, grey and white. Is this a good idea?

Bad behaviour

Adults recall how they behaved at school

1,844 adults (18+) who attended Secondary School in the UK were surveyed about their experience of 'pranks' and their own misbehaviour when they were at school.

Sources and weblinks:
Source: School Days: the best days of your life?
Opinium Research, August 2013
www.opinium.co.uk

Which of the following school pranks, if any, were you on the receiving end of whilst at school?

■ Male ■ Female

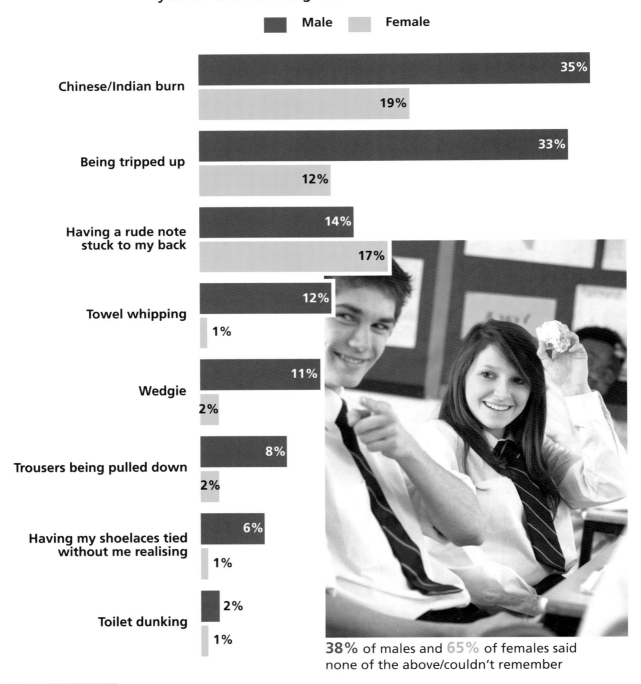

Chinese/Indian burn
- 35%
- 19%

Being tripped up
- 33%
- 12%

Having a rude note stuck to my back
- 14%
- 17%

Towel whipping
- 12%
- 1%

Wedgie
- 11%
- 2%

Trousers being pulled down
- 8%
- 2%

Having my shoelaces tied without me realising
- 6%
- 1%

Toilet dunking
- 2%
- 1%

38% of males and 65% of females said none of the above/couldn't remember

Which of the following, if any, is the most disobedient thing(s) you have done at Secondary School?

(You can select up to 3 options)

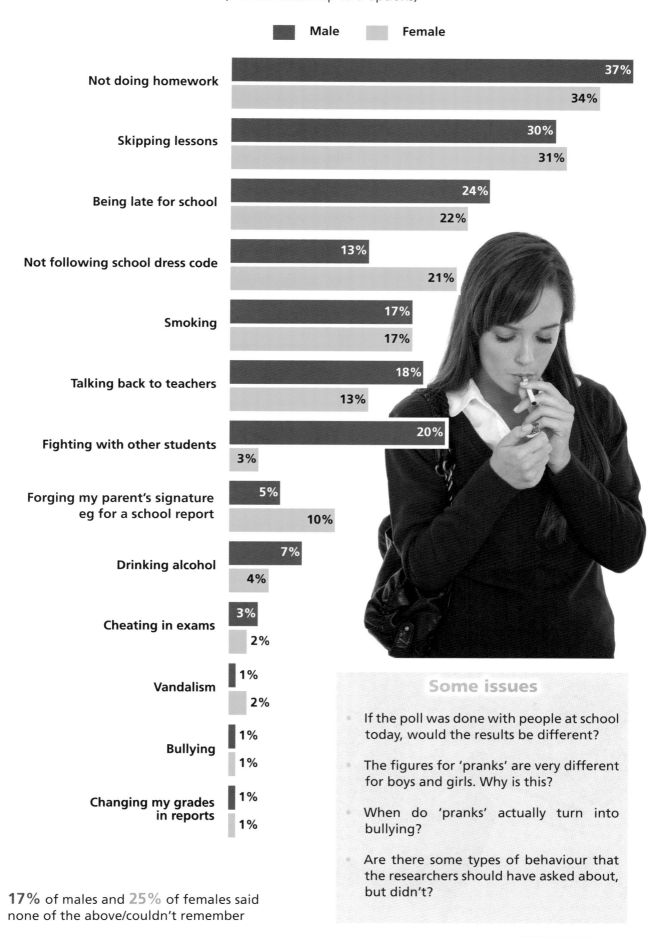

Male ■ **Female** ☐

Not doing homework
- Male: 37%
- Female: 34%

Skipping lessons
- Male: 30%
- Female: 31%

Being late for school
- Male: 24%
- Female: 22%

Not following school dress code
- Male: 13%
- Female: 21%

Smoking
- Male: 17%
- Female: 17%

Talking back to teachers
- Male: 18%
- Female: 13%

Fighting with other students
- Male: 20%
- Female: 3%

Forging my parent's signature eg for a school report
- Male: 5%
- Female: 10%

Drinking alcohol
- Male: 7%
- Female: 4%

Cheating in exams
- Male: 3%
- Female: 2%

Vandalism
- Male: 1%
- Female: 2%

Bullying
- Male: 1%
- Female: 1%

Changing my grades in reports
- Male: 1%
- Female: 1%

Some issues

- If the poll was done with people at school today, would the results be different?

- The figures for 'pranks' are very different for boys and girls. Why is this?

- When do 'pranks' actually turn into bullying?

- Are there some types of behaviour that the researchers should have asked about, but didn't?

17% of males and **25%** of females said none of the above/couldn't remember

Private schools

Opinions about the advantages of private schools

A YouGov survey for Prospect magazine of 1,620 GB adults in June/July 2013 examined attitudes towards private education. A further survey of 2,210 UK adults by YouGov for a private bank looked at the influence of cost.

Sources and weblinks:
Source: Education, privilege and fairness, YouGov; Private Schools vs state schools – is it simply about the cost, Duncan Lawrie Private Banking
www.yougov.co.uk
www.duncanlawrie.com

On average, pupils at private schools obtain higher A-level grades than pupils at state schools. From what you know, how do you assess each of these factors?

Net scores*

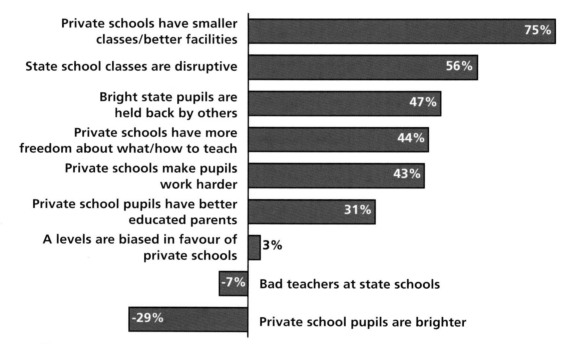

Factor	Net score
Private schools have smaller classes/better facilities	75%
State school classes are disruptive	56%
Bright state pupils are held back by others	47%
Private schools have more freedom about what/how to teach	44%
Private schools make pupils work harder	43%
Private school pupils have better educated parents	31%
A levels are biased in favour of private schools	3%
Bad teachers at state schools	-7%
Private school pupils are brighter	-29%

*Respondents could choose:
- true and an extremely important factor
- true and a fairly important factor
- true but only a minor factor
- not true; or
- don't know.

The net scores were calculated by adding the 'true and extremely or fairly important' scores then subtracting the 'not true' scores.

Which of these statements comes closest to your opinions?

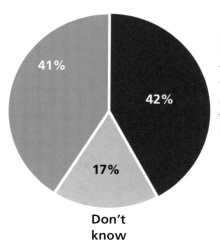

On balance, private schools harm Britain:
they reinforce privilege and social divisions, give children from better-off families an unfair advantage and undermine the state school system

41%

42%

17%

Don't know

On balance, private schools benefit Britain:
they provide many pupils with a good education, and are beacons of excellence that help to raise standards in state schools

A significantly higher proportion of pupils from private schools than from state schools gain admission to Britain's top universities.

In general do you think this is ...

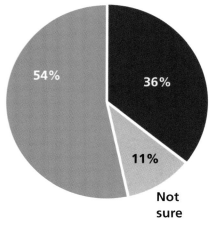

Unreasonable?
Top universities should do far more to offset the biases in the school system and find talented pupils in state schools

54%

36%

11%

Not sure

Reasonable?
Top universities should insist on maintaining their standards and choose the applicants with the best A-level results

---

The research for the bank found that, if money was not a consideration, 32% of people would send their children to private school. 81% of these said they thought these schools offer a better education.

Parents currently sending their children to private school spent on average £15,000 a year per child.

However, 50% of people said that they would still prefer to send their children to a state school, money or no money. 60% of this group said they felt their children would benefit from mixing with others from all walks of life.

Some issues

- Do you agree that smaller classes and better facilities are the most important factor in giving private school pupils better results.

- Do you think something should be done to make the chances of private and state school pupils more equal.

- Why are universities being encouraged to accept more state pupils?

See also Student numbers p60 and Essential Articles 2014, School fees buy more than good grades, p60

Student numbers

The number of people entering university has continued to fall - and there is evidence that the least privileged students have the lowest chance

UCAS provides figures for the number of applicants accepted each year into UK universities.

The Department for Business Innovation and Skills analysed the background of people progressing to university.

Sources and weblinks:
Source: UCAS Data Summary; Widening Participation in Higher Education, Department for Business, Innovation and Skills © Crown copyright 2013
www.ucas.com/data-analysis
www.gov.uk/bis

Number of university applications and acceptances, UK

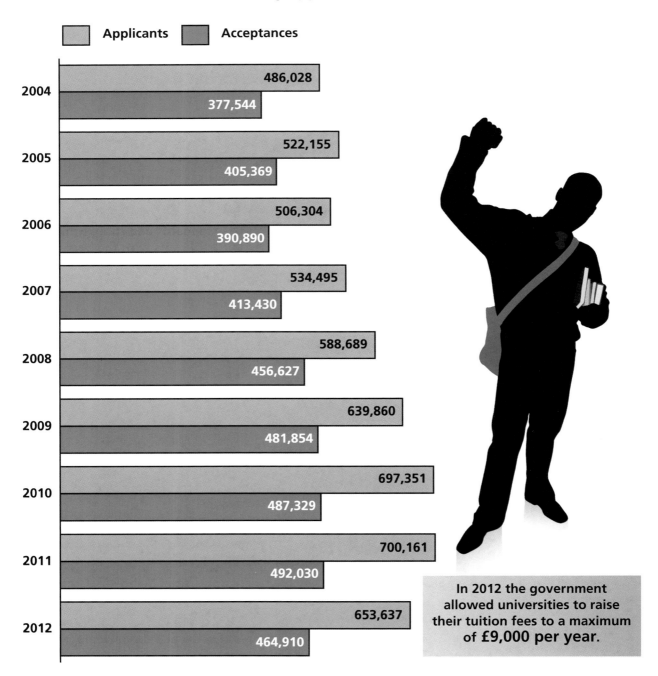

Applicants   Acceptances

2004
486,028
377,544

2005
522,155
405,369

2006
506,304
390,890

2007
534,495
413,430

2008
588,689
456,627

2009
639,860
481,854

2010
697,351
487,329

2011
700,161
492,030

2012
653,637
464,910

In 2012 the government allowed universities to raise their tuition fees to a maximum of £9,000 per year.

A level students who entered Higher Education by age 19

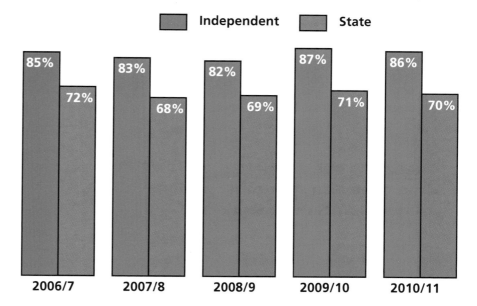

Independent | State

85% 72% 83% 68% 82% 69% 87% 71% 86% 70%

2006/7   2007/8   2008/9   2009/10   2010/11

The figures show that students from independent schools are much more successful than those from 'ordinary' state schools in accessing Higher Education.

A level students who entered the most selective institutions by age 19

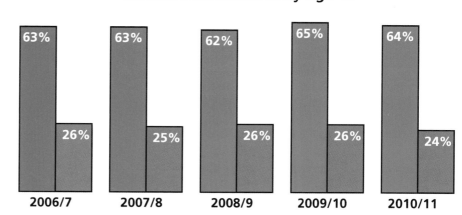

Independent school pupils are much more likely to enter the most prestigious universities.

The gap between independent and state sectors appears to have increased over time.

63% 26% 63% 25% 62% 26% 65% 26% 64% 24%

2006/7   2007/8   2008/9   2009/10   2010/11

Of all state school pupils who went into Higher Education **only 7%** came from the most deprived group (measured as pupils receiving Free School Meals).

Some issues

- Is the fall in student numbers caused only by the increase in fees or are there other factors?

- Why do you think more independent school students gain access to Higher Education and particularly the most selective institutions?

- What, if anything, can be done to help the least privileged students gain access to Higher Education?

See also Private schools p58, Essential Articles 2014, School fees buy more than good grades, p60 and Oxford and Camridge need to tackle race issues head-on, p62

Key subjects

The Higher Education Funding Council for England (HEFCE) has the responsibility of supporting teaching and research in key subjects. These include Chemistry, Mathematics, Physics and Modern Foreign Languages at university level. GCE A level entries show the trend for these subjects within schools.

Sources and weblinks:
Source: The Higher Education Funding Council for England (HEFCE), Joint Council for Qualifications
www.hefce.ac.uk
www.jcq.org.uk

There has been concern for some time about numbers of students in certain subjects

Certain subjects were classified as strategically important and vulnerable and therefore in need of support to increase student numbers. In most cases that support seems to have helped increase the take-up of university places.

In 2012-13 there was a **6%** drop in the total number of students accepting places, but the Science, Technology, Engineering and Maths (known as STEM subjects) only dropped by **3%**. Modern Foreign Languages, however, saw a decline of **9%**.

Numbers of students taking up university places in selected shortage subjects

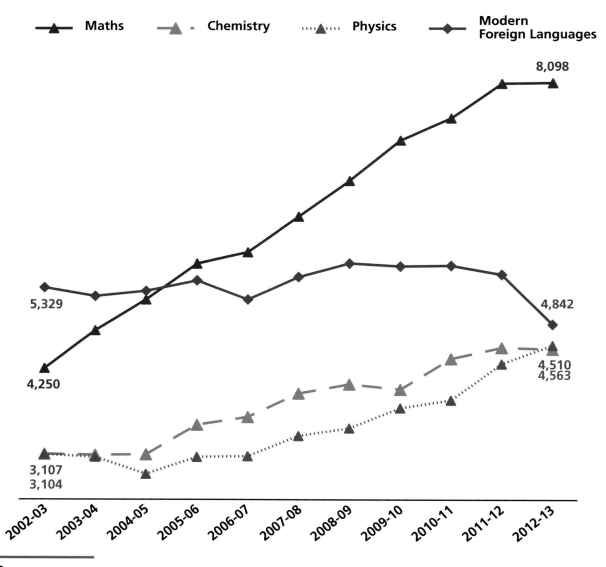

— Maths   — Chemistry   ···· Physics   ◆ Modern Foreign Languages

8,098

5,329

4,842

4,250

4,510
4,563

3,107
3,104

2002-03 2003-04 2004-05 2005-06 2006-07 2007-08 2008-09 2009-10 2010-11 2011-12 2012-13

The number of students accepting places in French studies fell by 15% from 2011/12 to 2012/13.

In German the fall in the same years was 31%.

The number of A level entrants in French and German also fell between 2012 and 2013, while entries in science subjects increased.

Percentage change in numbers sitting A level exams 2012 to 2013 (selected subjects)

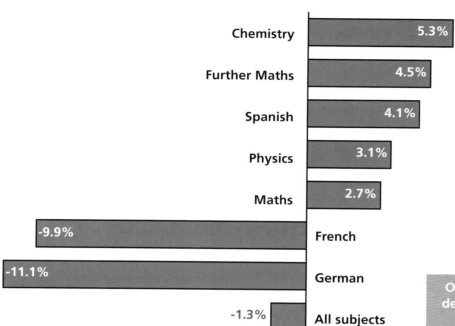

Subject	Percentage change
Chemistry	5.3%
Further Maths	4.5%
Spanish	4.1%
Physics	3.1%
Maths	2.7%
French	-9.9%
German	-11.1%
All subjects	-1.3%

One reason for the decline in uptake of language A levels might be a concern about harder marking.

A* grades were awarded to 6.9% of students in French, German and Spanish compared with 8.4% in Physics, Chemistry and Biology.

Some issues

- Why is it a problem if some subjects do not attract students?

- What influences people's choices at A level and university level?

- If you want to encourage people to study a subject, what should you do and when?

Overseas students

Young people who come to the UK to study contribute to the economy

4.3 million students worldwide are enrolled in Higher Education courses outside their own country. The proportion of these who study in the UK has grown and should continue to grow.

Sources and weblinks:

Source: International Education: Global Growth and Prosperity, Department for Business, Innovation and Skills © Crown copyright 2013; Education at a Glance: OECD Indicators, Organisation for Economic Cooperation and Development, 2013
www.gov.uk/bis
www.oecd.org/edu/eag

Most popular destinations for international Higher Education students
(% of global total 2011)

United States	16.5%
United Kingdom	13.0%
Germany	6.3%
France	6.2%
Australia	6.1%
Canada	4.7%

The **United States'** share of international students has fallen from **23%** in 2000. The **UK's** share increased by **2 percentage points** over the same period.

In 2011/12 **435,000** overseas students studying at university level in the UK paid **£3.9 billion** in fees and **£6.3 billion** in living expenses.

Some issues

- Why is the UK an attractive destination for foreign students?

- Why is the US more appealing?

- Besides money, what benefits do foreign students bring to the UK?

- If you wanted to study abroad, where would you choose and why?

Environmental issues

Beach litter

Our passion for plastic is leaving a legacy of litter on Britain's beaches

Every year the Marine Conservation Society organise the Beachwatch Big Weekend, the only national beach litter clean up and survey of its kind in the UK.

Almost 3,500 volunteers cleaned up over 90km of the UK's coastline.

Sources and weblinks:
Source: Beachwatch Big Weekend 2012 – Marine Conservation Society
www.mcsuk.org/beachwatch

Litter is filling the oceans and washing up on beaches....

- it kills wildlife
- it is a health hazard
- it costs millions to clear up

What happens to our rubbish?

- More and more organisations and individuals are putting marine creatures at risk without realising it. Balloon and lantern releases over land eventually drift down into the sea and end up in the gullets of seabirds, turtles and dolphins who mistake them for food.

- Marine wildlife gets entangled in litter and accidentally ingests it. Turtles mistake plastic bags for jellyfish and the bags block their stomachs, often leading to death from starvation.

- Seabirds mistake floating plastic litter for food and over 90% of fulmars found dead around the North Sea have plastic in their stomachs.

- Face scrubs, masks and peels contain tiny plastic particles. When it is rinsed off, it goes down the drain and eventually into the sea where it contributes to the 'plastic soup' problem. Microplastic particles are now found inside animals that filter water in order to feed, such as flamingos, clams, and sponges and amongst sand grains on our beaches.

During the Beachwatch Big Weekend:

almost **240** beaches were cleaned	nearly **1,800** bin bags were filled	**181,978** items of litter were collected	**2,007** pieces of litter were found for every kilometre surveyed

Top 10 litter items found on our beaches per km

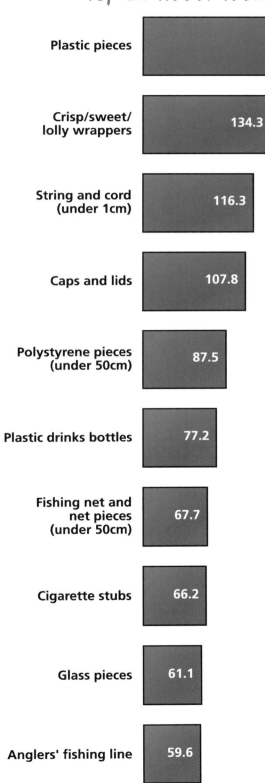

Plastic pieces	429.5
Crisp/sweet/lolly wrappers	134.3
String and cord (under 1cm)	116.3
Caps and lids	107.8
Polystyrene pieces (under 50cm)	87.5
Plastic drinks bottles	77.2
Fishing net and net pieces (under 50cm)	67.7
Cigarette stubs	66.2
Glass pieces	61.1
Anglers' fishing line	59.6

Plastic

Plastic litter on beaches has increased 135% since 1994. It never biodegrades, it just breaks down into small pieces but does not disappear.

The amount of plastic on our beaches rose by 3% in 2012 and made up almost 65% of all the litter found there.

Cigarettes

There was a 100% rise in the number of cigarette stubs found on beaches over the last year, with general smoking litter, including lighters and packets, increasing by 90%.

Where does it all come from?

Litter comes from many sources – the public, fishing activities, sewage pipes and shipping... but it is all preventable

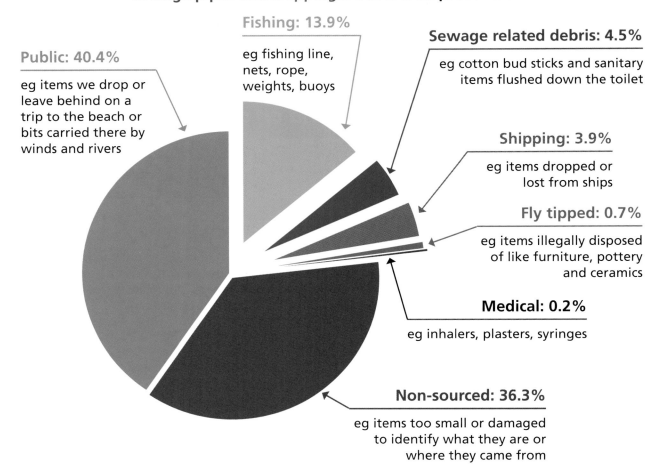

Fishing: 13.9%
eg fishing line, nets, rope, weights, buoys

Sewage related debris: 4.5%
eg cotton bud sticks and sanitary items flushed down the toilet

Public: 40.4%
eg items we drop or leave behind on a trip to the beach or bits carried there by winds and rivers

Shipping: 3.9%
eg items dropped or lost from ships

Fly tipped: 0.7%
eg items illegally disposed of like furniture, pottery and ceramics

Medical: 0.2%
eg inhalers, plasters, syringes

Non-sourced: 36.3%
eg items too small or damaged to identify what they are or where they came from

Beachwatch Volunteers

Diving for rubbish

In 2012, the British Sub Aqua Club took Beachwatch underwater – 358 volunteer divers at 67 sites collected 149 bags weighing 885kg which contained 4,618 pieces of litter.

"How fantastic to do something local whilst being part of something global and making a difference to such a precious habitat"

Lynn Allen, Beachwatch Volunteer

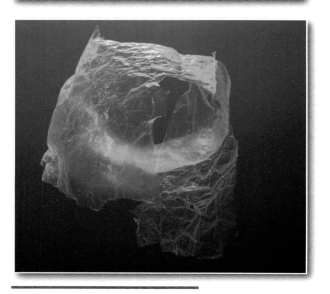

Some issues

• How can we reduce the amount of litter on our beaches and in our seas?

• In your opinion, why has the amount of plastic and smoking litter increased?

• Apart from collecting up some litter, does a survey like this serve any purpose?

See also Essential Articles 14, The truth is hard to swallow, p68

Natural environment

Spending time in the fresh air is keeping us healthy – both physically and mentally

A yearly survey of 45,000 people in England gives a valuable insight into how people enjoy the outdoors – who is using it, where we visit, what we do when we're out there and how it affects our behaviour, attitudes and general wellbeing.

NB Figures may not add up to 100% due to rounding or because more than one answer could be given

Sources and weblinks:

*Source: Monitor of Engagement with the Natural Environment 4th annual report
Infographic: TNS
www.naturalengland.org.uk
www.tnsglobal.com*

Who visits and how often?

The English adult population made approximately **2.85 billion visits** to the outdoors between March 2012 and February 2013 (Year 4 of the survey).

The proportion of people taking at least one visit to the outdoors in the previous week for health and exercise has **increased** from **34%** in 2009/10 (Year 1 of the survey) to **44%** in Year 4 (2012/13).

The population groups most likely to make visits to the natural environment are those aged 25-64, those living in rural areas, people in employment and those in the better off socio-economic groups.

In 2012/13:

Places visited

46%
Countryside

43%
Towns/cities

7%
Seaside resorts

3%
Other coastal areas

Top activities

1.4 bn
visits
Walking with a dog

769m
visits
Walking without a dog

235m
visits
Playing with children

173m
visits
Eating/ drinking out

Top 3 specific destinations visited

25% of all visits were to parks in towns/cities

16% were to paths/cycleways/bridleways

13% were to woodlands/forests

" *It is clear that visits to the countryside and local green spaces are playing an increasingly important role in providing health and exercise opportunities for millions of people each year.* "

Dr Tim Hill
Director for Evidence at Natural England

Benefits of visiting the outdoors

98%
enjoyed their visit to the natural environment

88%
felt refreshed and revitalised

85%
agreed that it made them feel calm and relaxed

82%
took time to appreciate their surroundings

Motivations and barriers to visiting the outdoors

Top motivations

47% exercising a dog

44% health/exercise

28% to relax and unwind

26% fresh air/pleasant weather

The greatest reported barriers

24% said they were too busy at work

15% said they were too busy at home

Generally, motivation varies by age

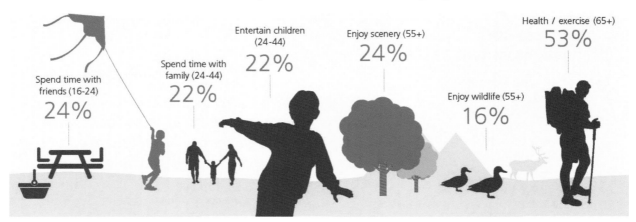

Spend time with friends (16-24)
24%

Spend time with family (24-44)
22%

Entertain children (24-44)
22%

Enjoy scenery (55+)
24%

Enjoy wildlife (55+)
16%

Health / exercise (65+)
53%

Spending on visits

These visits are good for the economy too. Although **73%** of visits are free, with no spending at all, the remainder have a big economic impact.

27%
of visits involved spending

An average of
£27
was spent during these visits

This amounts to around
£21 billion
spend in total

Breakdown of how every £1 is spent on visits to the outdoors

Food & drink **54p**

Fuel **14p**

Admission fees **9p**

Gifts / souvenirs **6p**

Hire / purchase equipment **4p**

Other **13p**

While only **10%** of all visits are to seaside resorts and other coastline, **22%** of all spending takes place during those visits.

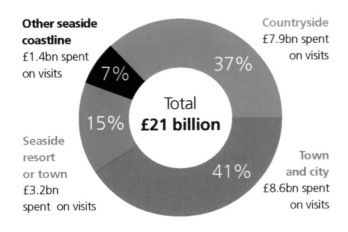

Other seaside coastline
£1.4bn spent on visits

7%

Countryside
£7.9bn spent on visits

37%

Total
£21 billion

Seaside resort or town
£3.2bn spent on visits

15%

41%

Town and city
£8.6bn spent on visits

Some issues

- Why do you think there are fewer visits to the coast but a higher proportion of spending there?

- What would be your own favourite place to visit?

- What might stop you from visiting the 'great outdoors'?

See also Importance of woodland p72

Importance of woodland

Public attitudes to forestry and woodland

1,927 UK adults, aged 16 or over, were asked about their visits to forests or woodlands in the last few years: what they did there, how they thought climate change was affecting trees and how trees could be protected.

Sources and weblinks:

Source: UK Public Opinion of Forestry survey © Crown copyright 2013
www.forestry.gov.uk

Visits & how often

66% had visited forests or woodlands in the last few years for walks, picnics or other recreation.

Of those who had visited woodlands:

- 73% said that they had visited at least once a month during summer 2012
- 42% said they visited at least once a month during winter 2012/13

Top ten woodland activities taken part in during their visit

(More than one answer could be given)

Activity	%
Exercised eg walking, running, mountain biking	69%
Relaxed or spent time thinking	32%
Played with the children	32%
Had a picnic or barbeque	30%
Dog walking	30%
Watched nature	29%
Visited a café	28%
Visited an historic sight	21%
Followed a trail	13%
Enjoyed sculpture or arts & crafts	9%

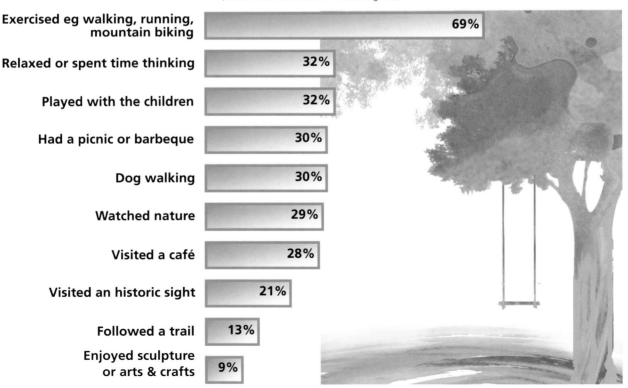

Main reasons respondents thought woodlands and forests were important to the public

(% of respondents who agree or strongly agree with the following statements)

Important places for wildlife	93%
Places where people can relax and de-stress	91%
People can have fun and enjoy themselves	91%
They are places where people can exercise and keep fit	89%
They make areas nicer places to live	87%
People can learn about the environment	87%

Main ways respondents thought forests and woodlands can impact on climate change

(% of respondents who agree or strongly agree with the following statements)

Trees are good because they remove CO2 from the atmosphere and store it in wood	80%
Planting more trees can help us cope with climate change by providing shade and reducing the effects of flooding	72%
The UK could offset all its greenhouse gas emissions by planting more trees	55%
Cutting down forests and woodland makes climate change worse, even if they are replanted	55%

Some issues

- Do we have enough woodland and forest in the UK?

- Many people are concerned about the loss of woodlands. What is the most important reason for preserving them?

- When would removing woodland be the right thing to do?

See also Natural environment p69

Arctic melt

As the climate warms, Arctic sea ice is disappearing

Sea ice is frozen ocean water that melts each summer and refreezes each winter.

Arctic sea ice has long been recognised as a sensitive climate indicator. It already affects wildlife.

Sources and weblinks:
Source: National Snow and Ice Data Center (NSIDC); World Wildlife Fund(WWF)
http://nsidc.org
www.wwf.org.uk
wwf.panda.org

Why is sea ice important?

Sea ice has a bright surface so it **REFLECTS 80%** of the sunlight that strikes it back into space. This keeps the Arctic region cool and moderates the global climate.

But as sea ice melts in the summer, the darker surface of the ocean is exposed which **ABSORBS 90%** of the sunlight.

What is sea ice extent?

Extent is a measure of how far the edge of the ice reaches.

Maximum and minimum sea ice extent

The Arctic ice cap grows to its annual maximum each winter as the sun sets for several months and shrinks each summer to its annual minimum extent in September.

Record low

September Arctic sea extent has **declined by 13% per decade** since satellite records began in 1979.

On 16 September 2012, Arctic sea ice fell to **3.41 million square km** - the **lowest extent** ever recorded.

Downward trend

This year's summer was cooler than previous ones which helped to slow the melting but despite these lower temperatures, the ice extent still **fell well below the long-term average.** On 13 September 2013, Arctic sea ice reached its minimum extent of around **5.10* million square km.**

*This figure is provisional as the wind may push ice floes together which will reduce the ice extent even more

The extent and thickness of the summer sea ice in the Arctic has shown a dramatic decline over the past 30 years

Photo courtesy of NASA/Kathryn Hansen and the National Snow and Ice Data Center, University of Colorado, Boulder

Scientists watch from the deck of the U.S. Coast Guard Cutter Healy as it cuts through ice in the Arctic Ocean

Arctic sea ice extent, millions of square km

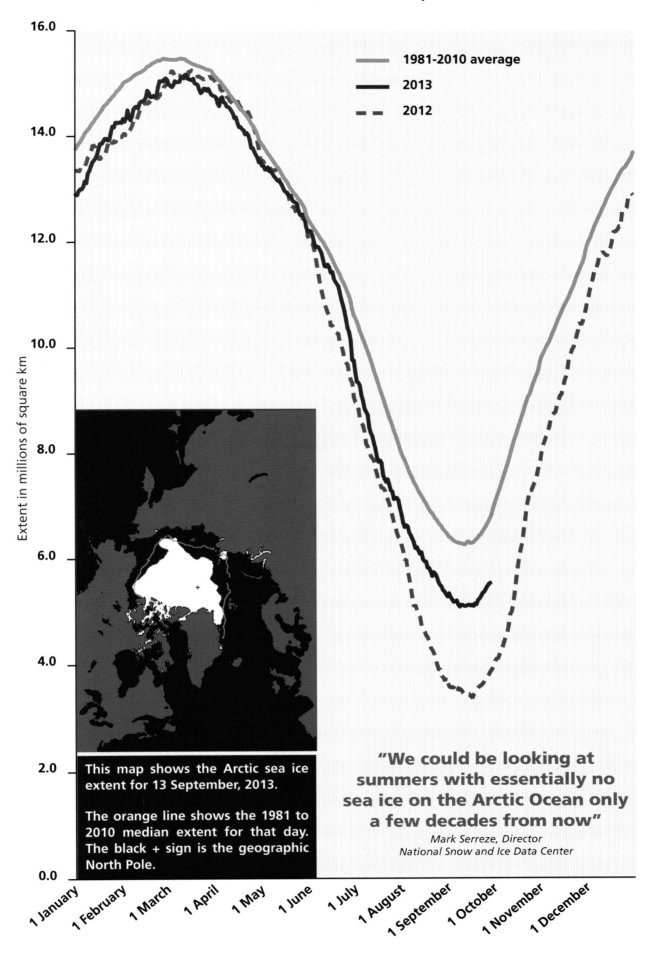

Extent in millions of square km

1981-2010 average

2013

2012

16.0
14.0
12.0
10.0
8.0
6.0
4.0
2.0
0.0

1 January · 1 February · 1 March · 1 April · 1 May · 1 June · 1 July · 1 August · 1 September · 1 October · 1 November · 1 December

This map shows the Arctic sea ice extent for 13 September, 2013.

The orange line shows the 1981 to 2010 median extent for that day. The black + sign is the geographic North Pole.

"We could be looking at summers with essentially no sea ice on the Arctic Ocean only a few decades from now"

Mark Serreze, Director
National Snow and Ice Data Center

Current polar bear populations

There are an estimated **20,000** to **25,000** wild polar bears worldwide
living in **19** sub-populations.

The threat to polar bears

The Arctic is the home of the polar bear. They rely on sea ice as a platform in hunting for seals, their main prey.

Fewer than **2%** of a polar bear's hunts are successful but they use up a lot of energy in the process. The bears need to eat enough to store energy as fat for the summer and autumn, when food is scarce.

As the ice melts, the seals become harder to find and the bears don't have enough fat reserves to remain healthy during the ice-free season on land.

This affects their ability to reproduce. Their litters are decreasing in size and scientists have also found that the main cause of death for cubs is either lack of food or lack of fat on nursing mothers.

Polar bears could be gone from most of their current areas within 100 years.

A 2011 study found that **7 of the 19** sub-populations of polar bears were **declining**, with trends in **two** linked to the reduction in sea ice.

Status of Polar bears

International: Vulnerable

Greenland/Denmark: Vulnerable

Norway: Vulnerable

Russia: Uncertain, Rare, and Rehabilitated/Rehabilitating

US: Threatened

60-80% of polar bears are in Canada where their status is listed as a Species of special concern

Some issues

- Would it matter if polar bears became extinct?

- How is the rest of the world affected by the melting sea ice?

- Can anything be done to stop the ice melting?

See also Essential Articles 2014, Greenland reaps benefits of global warming, p68

Family & relationships

Conceptions

There is a general trend towards fewer conceptions amongst the youngest age groups and more in the older groups

The rates shown here count all conceptions whatever the outcome (eg live birth, still birth or termination).

In 2011, teenage pregnancies were at the lowest level since records began. This is important as teenage pregnancy and early motherhood can be linked with poor educational achievement, poor physical and mental health, social isolation and poverty.

Sources and weblinks:
Source: Conceptions in England and Wales
© Crown copyright 2013
www.ons.gov.uk

Annual conception rate, England and Wales
(conceptions per thousand women in each age group)

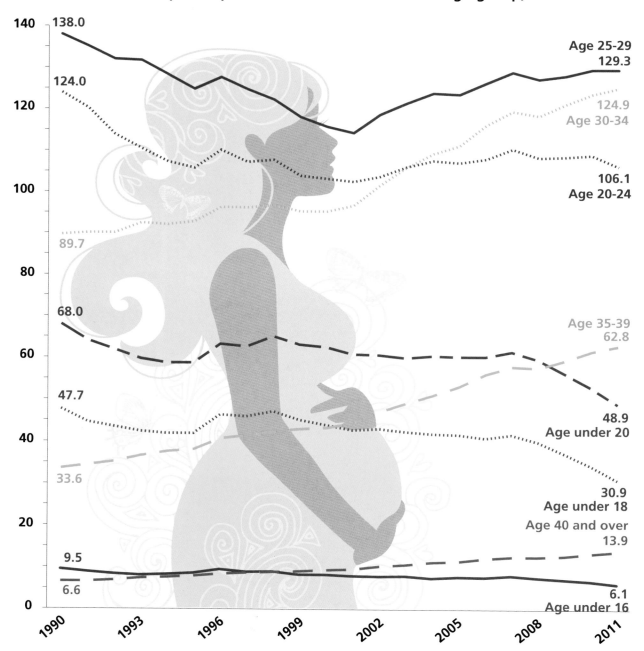

Age 25-29 — 138.0 ... 129.3
Age 30-34 — 124.0 ... 124.9
Age 20-24 — 89.7 ... 106.1
Age 35-39 — 62.8
Age under 20 — 68.0 ... 48.9
Age under 18 — 47.7 ... 30.9
Age 40 and over — 33.6 ... 13.9
Age under 16 — 9.5 / 6.6 ... 6.1

1990 1993 1996 1999 2002 2005 2008 2011

The changes in conception rate over time can be seen more clearly by using 1990 as a base ie 1990 = 100%

% changes in conception rates for each age group

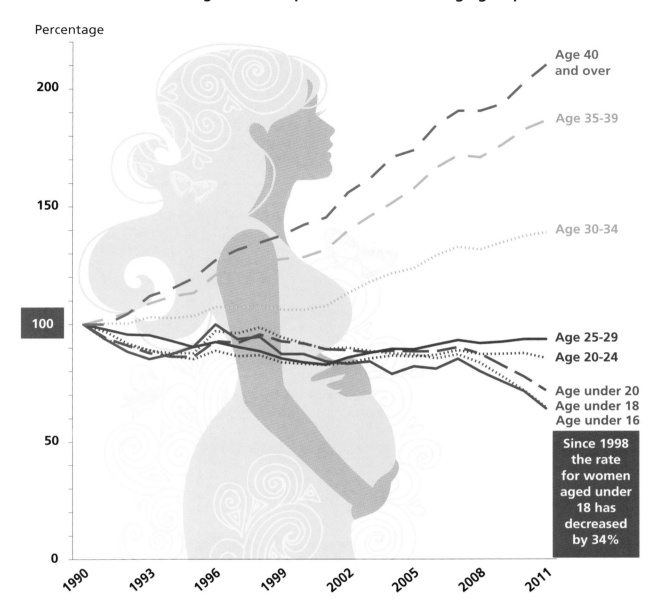

Percentage

- Age 40 and over
- Age 35-39
- Age 30-34
- Age 25-29
- Age 20-24
- Age under 20
- Age under 18
- Age under 16

200
150
100
50
0

1990 1993 1996 1999 2002 2005 2008 2011

Since 1998 the rate for women aged under 18 has decreased by 34%

The conception rate for women aged 40 and over has more than doubled since 1990.

Some reasons for this could be that more women are:

- participating in higher education;
- getting married or forming partnerships later;
- establishing a career, getting on the housing ladder and ensuring financial stability before starting a family.

Some issues

- The charts show a different trend for different age groups. Why do you think the trends for the under-thirties and over-thirties are so different?

- What conclusions could you draw from the under-twenties conception rate?

- Do you think these trends will continue?

Multiple maternities

Multiple births that arise from a single pregnancy are counted as one maternity.

The number of maternities therefore shows the number of women having babies (including stillbirths) rather than the number of babies born.

Since 1976 the multiple birth rate has increased for all ages but most notably for women aged 30 and over in England and Wales

Sources and weblinks:

Source: Births in England and Wales by Characteristics of Birth; Childhood, Infant & Perinatal Mortality in England & Wales © Crown copyright 2013
www.ons.gov.uk

In 2011:

- **11,330** women gave birth to **twins**;
- **172** to **triplets**; and
- **3** to **quads and above**.

These multiple maternities include both live births and stillbirths.

The multiple maternity rate increased to **16.1** per 1,000 women giving birth, compared with **15.7** in 2010.

Since 2001 the multiple maternity rate has increased by **8.8%**.

Maternities with multiple births by age of mother, per thousands total maternities

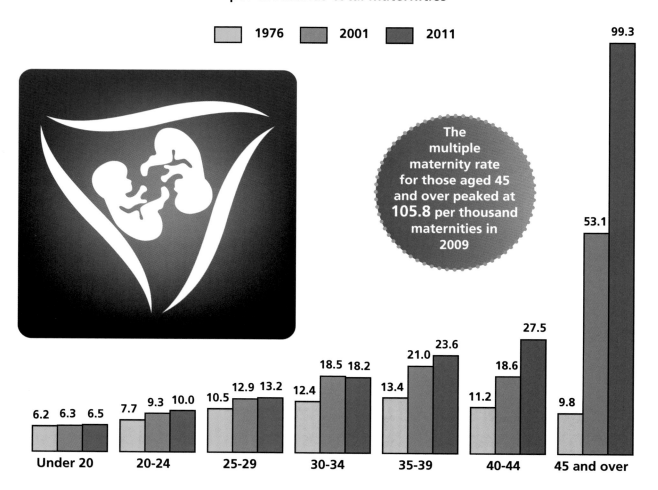

| | 1976 | 2001 | 2011 |

The multiple maternity rate for those aged 45 and over peaked at **105.8** per thousand maternities in 2009

Age	1976	2001	2011
Under 20	6.2	6.3	6.5
20-24	7.7	9.3	10.0
25-29	10.5	12.9	13.2
30-34	12.4	18.5	18.2
35-39	13.4	21.0	23.6
40-44	11.2	18.6	27.5
45 and over	9.8	53.1	99.3

Birthweight

On average, multiple births tend to have lower birthweights than singletons which is one reason why the infant death rate is around **five times higher** for multiple births than for singleton births –**19.5** deaths per 1,000 compared to **3.8** deaths per 1,000 live births.

Multiple pregnancies are also linked with a higher risk of stillbirth, infant death and child disability.

Infant death rate for babies born in 2010, England and Wales

(Rate per 1,000 live births)

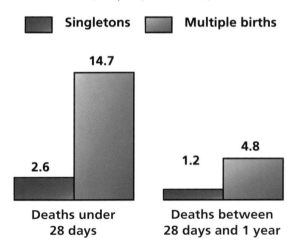

■ **Singletons**   ■ **Multiple births**

14.7

2.6

Deaths under 28 days

1.2   4.8

Deaths between 28 days and 1 year

IVF (In Vitro Fertilisation)

Although multiple births can happen naturally, many occur as a result of fertility treatment.

On average, **25%** of IVF pregnancies result in either twins or triplets compared with **1%** for women who conceive naturally.

With approximately **11,000** IVF babies being born each year this contributes greatly to the multiple birth rate.

Some issues

- Why does the rate of multiple births increase with the age of the mother?

- Why do you think the number of multiple births has increased?

- Why might there be more stillbirths and infant deaths in the multiple group?

- Does it make any difference to society as a whole that there are more twins and triplets than ever before?

Adoptions

It is possible that the increased number of adoptions in 2012 could be the result of the drive to improve the adoption process in England and in Wales. However, many new regulations were not yet in force when the statistics were collected.

Sources and weblinks:

Source: Adoptions in England and Wales, August 2013 Office for National Statistics; General Register Office for Scotland; Northern Ireland Statistics and Research Agency © Crown copyright 2013
www.ons.gov.uk
www.gro-scotland.gov.uk
www.nisra.gov.uk

2012 saw the largest annual increase in adoptions for 15 years. However there was a decline in adoptions of some age groups

Number of Adoptions 1998 - 2012, England and Wales

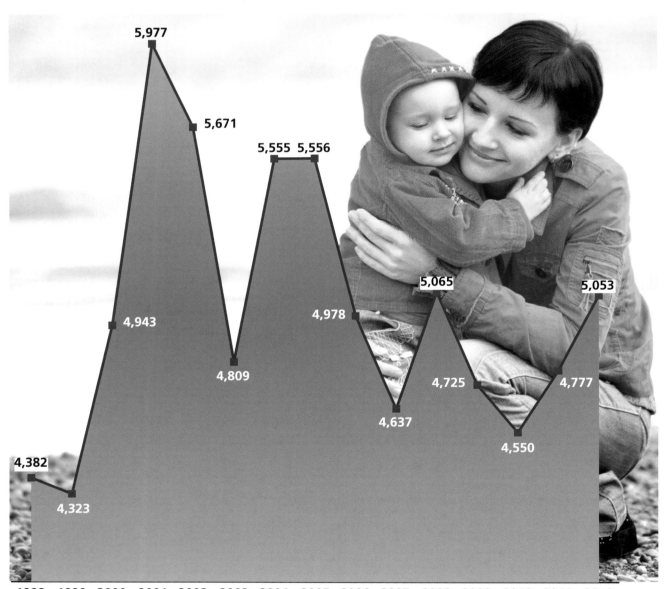

4,382	4,323	4,943	5,977	5,671	4,809	5,555	5,556	4,978	4,637	5,065	4,725	4,550	4,777	5,053
1998	1999	2000	2001	2002	2003	2004	2005	2006	2007	2008	2009	2010	2011	2012

In Scotland there were **496** adoptions in 2011 and **495** in 2012.

In Northern Ireland there were **116** adoptions in 2010 and **104** in 2011 (the last year for which figures were available).

Percentage of adoptions by age group 1998 - 2012, England and Wales

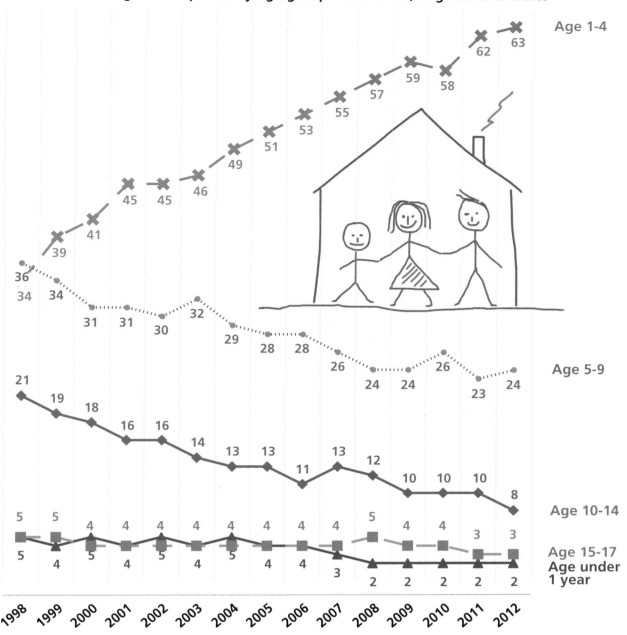

Age 1-4

63
62
59
58
57
55
53
51
49
46
45
45
41
39
36
34   34
31   31   30   32   29   28   28   26   24   24   26   23   24

Age 5-9

21
19
18
16   16   14   13   13   11   13   12   10   10   10   8

Age 10-14

5   5   4   4   4   4   4   4   4   4   5   4   4   3   3

Age 15-17

5   4   5   4   5   4   5   4   4   3   2   2   2   2   2

Age under 1 year

1998 1999 2000 2001 2002 2003 2004 2005 2006 2007 2008 2009 2010 2011 2012

The government proposes to speed up the adoption process by:

- **not trying to achieve a near-perfect ethnic match;**
- **using the national Adoption Register to match children and adopters wherever they live;**
- **placing children with potential adopters before the formal court proceedings;**
- **reducing the training/assessment process to six months;**
- **using a fast-track for people who have adopted before or want to adopt their foster child.**

Some issues

- Is it a good idea to make the adoption process shorter and easier?

- Why do you think the percentages of 10-14 year olds being adopted are declining?

- How can more people be encouraged to adopt and foster?

- How would it affect you if your family adopted or fostered?

Trends in family size

Childlessness and fertility patterns over the last 70 years in England and Wales

In order to measure whether fertility rates were changing over time, women born in 1939 and 1966 (the most recent group to have finished having children) were compared. The figures focus on women of childbearing age, 16 to 45.

They show that women are having children later, more women are remaining childless and average family size is decreasing.

Sources and weblinks:
Source: Office for National Statistics
© Crown copyright 2013
www.ons.gov.uk

Average family size for women who have completed their families (age 45yrs)

Year of birth of woman	Average completed family size	Number of live-born children %				
		0	1	2	3	4+
1939	2.36	12	13	35	22	18
1966	1.91	20	14	38	18	10

Family size

To get an idea of recent trends we can look at the average number of children women have had up to their 30th birthday.

Those born in **1939** had **1.87 children** by their 30th birthday compared with the **1966** group of women who had **1.17 children** on average by the same age.

Overall, women born in the 1960s and 1970s have had fewer children by age 30 than previous generations. They are delaying having children for reasons including:

- being in higher education
- forming partnerships or marrying later
- establishing a career, getting on the housing ladder and ensuring financial stability before starting a family.

From 1958 onwards, the average number of children per woman is **fewer than two** mainly due to more women remaining childless.

One way of comparing the proportion of women who had at least one child is to imagine the women as school year groups of 100 girls born in each year: **1966** – the most recent group of women to finish having children – and **1939** – a group equivalent to their mothers.

Number of women who have had at least one child

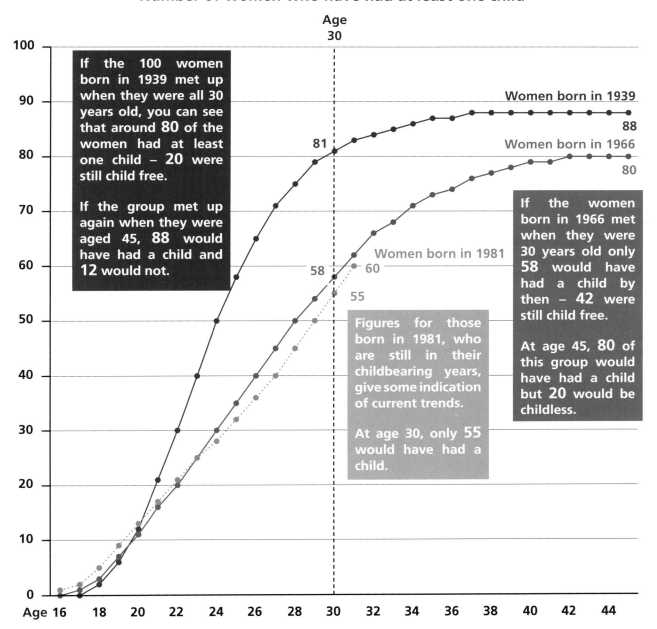

If the 100 women born in 1939 met up when they were all 30 years old, you can see that around 80 of the women had at least one child – 20 were still child free.

If the group met up again when they were aged 45, 88 would have had a child and 12 would not.

Women born in 1939

88

Women born in 1966

80

Women born in 1981

If the women born in 1966 met when they were 30 years old only 58 would have had a child by then – 42 were still child free.

At age 45, 80 of this group would have had a child but 20 would be childless.

Figures for those born in 1981, who are still in their childbearing years, give some indication of current trends.

At age 30, only 55 would have had a child.

Age 30

81
58 60
55

Age 16   18   20   22   24   26   28   30   32   34   36   38   40   42   44

The average age at which women have children has been increasing

When the **1939** group were **aged 22**, **30%** of them had had one or more babies. When they were **aged 24**, this increased to **50%**, and **75%** by **age 28**.

The **1966** group were **aged 24** when **30%** had had one or more babies. This group only reached **50%** at **age 28**, and **75%** by **age 37** – nine years later than the 1939 group.

Family snapshot

Families appear to be getting smaller

These figures show the current make up of families in the UK by the number of dependent* children they have – families may go on to have more children later.

*Dependent children are those aged under 16 living with at least one parent, or aged 16 to 18 in full-time education, excluding all children who have a spouse, partner or child living in the household.

Sources and weblinks:

Source: Family size in 2012, Office for National Statistics © Crown copyright 2013
www.ons.gov.uk

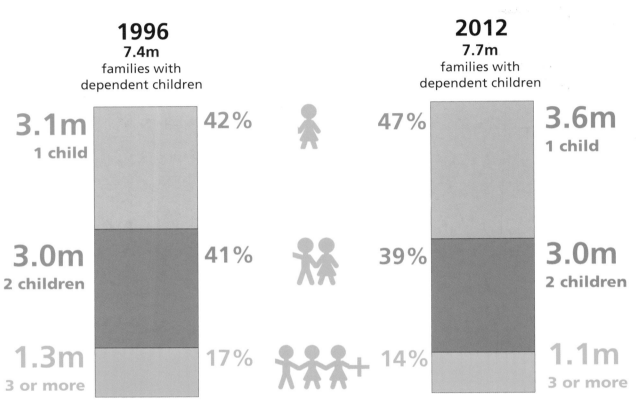

1996
7.4m
families with dependent children

3.1m 1 child — 42%

3.0m 2 children — 41%

1.3m 3 or more — 17%

2012
7.7m
families with dependent children

47% — **3.6m** 1 child

39% — **3.0m** 2 children

14% — **1.1m** 3 or more

1996 and 2012 are the earliest and latest years for which comparable figures are available

Average number of dependent children

Married or civil partnered couples had a higher average number of dependent children in their families than other family types – **1.8** dependent children per family compared with **1.7** for all families.

Lone parent families and **co-habiting couples** had **1.6** dependent children on average.

Employment of parents in the UK

Families with one or two dependent children are more likely to have at least one employed parent than those with three or more dependent children.

% of families with at least one working parent:

 COUPLES with
1 or 2 dependent children **95%**

 COUPLES with
3 or more
dependent children **87%**

 LONE PARENTS with
1 or 2 dependent children **62%**

 LONE PARENTS with
3 or more
dependent children **38%**

This graph shows the greater challenge of combining work with childcare with three or more children compared with one or two.

It also shows that living with a partner makes it easier to work and to share childcare responsibilities.

Research shows that as the age of the youngest child in the family increases so does the opportunity for the mother in the family to be in work and the gap narrows between the employment rates for mothers with a partner living in the household and those without a partner.

Some issues

- Why might average family size be decreasing?

- What factors would make it harder to go out to work if you have more children?

- What is the ideal family size, in your opinion?

See also Trends in family size p84

Probability of divorce

Some things which affect how likely a couple are to get a divorce include:

- length of marriage
- age at marriage
- whether married before
- year of marriage

Sources and weblinks:
Source: Divorces in England and Wales - 2011
© Crown copyright 2013
www.ons.gov.uk

The average marriage is expected to last for 32 years

Length of marriage

For divorces granted in 2011, the average length of the marriage being ended was 11.5 years.

Whether married before

In 2011, 20% of men and 19% of women divorcing had already had a previous marriage end in divorce. These proportions have almost doubled since 1980, while the percentage of couples divorcing where this was the first marriage for both parties has generally declined.

Age at marriage

Research has shown that those who marry younger are more likely to divorce. For example if we look at women who married for the first time in 1976

- for those aged less than 20 when they married, 53% had divorced by their 30th anniversary

- if they were aged 30 to 34 when they married 23% had divorced by the same anniversary, and

- if they were aged 45 to 49 when they married 7% had divorced

Cumulative percentage of marriages ending in divorce

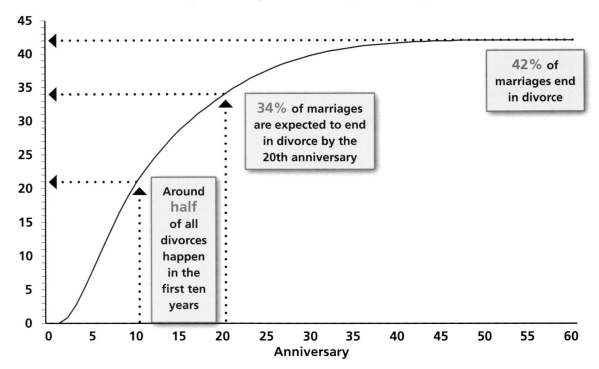

42% of marriages end in divorce

34% of marriages are expected to end in divorce by the 20th anniversary

Around half of all divorces happen in the first ten years

Anniversary

What is the probability of divorce?

Between the 4th and 8th anniversaries, the chance of divorce by next anniversary is over 3%

By the 26th anniversary, the chance of divorce by next anniversary falls to less than 1%

Y-axis: Percentage chance (0.0 to 3.5)
X-axis: Anniversary (0 to 50)

Year of marriage

The percentage of marriages ending in divorce has generally increased for those marrying between the early 1970s and the early 1990s. 22% of marriages in 1970 had ended by the 15th wedding anniversary, while in 1995 33% of marriages had ended by this time.

For people marrying since 2000, the percentage of marriages ending in divorce appears to be falling. This may be related to two factors:

- The age at which people first marry has been increasing, and those marrying when they are older have a lower risk of divorce.

- Because people often live together before getting married, this may mean that weaker relationships break up before progressing to marriage.

Some issues

- 42% of marriages end in divorce. Does that mean getting married should be made more difficult?

- Why would the age at which you get married influence your chance of divorce?

- Do you think the reasons given for the divorce rate falling after 2000 are valid ones?

Marriage

YouGov spoke to 1,701 GB adults to find out what traditions they thought were important when it comes to family and marriage.

Sources and weblinks:
Source: YouGov, British Brides Want Fairytale Weddings, July 2013
www.yougov.com

People are relaxed about marriage itself, but are attached to wedding traditions

Do you think it is acceptable or unacceptable for a couple to have children when they are not married?

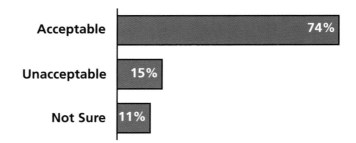

Acceptable	74%
Unacceptable	15%
Not Sure	11%

And whether or not it is acceptable, do you think is it better for a couple having children to be married or unmarried, or does it make no difference?

It's better for them to be married	51%
It's better for them to be unmarried	2%
It makes no difference they are equally good	45%
Not sure	2%

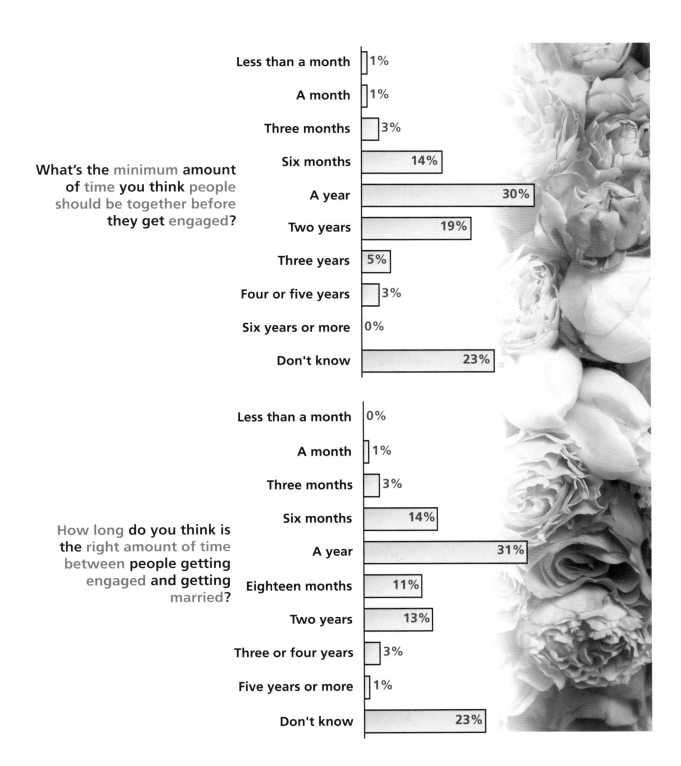

What's the minimum amount of time you think people should be together before they get engaged?

Less than a month	1%
A month	1%
Three months	3%
Six months	14%
A year	30%
Two years	19%
Three years	5%
Four or five years	3%
Six years or more	0%
Don't know	23%

How long do you think is the right amount of time between people getting engaged and getting married?

Less than a month	0%
A month	1%
Three months	3%
Six months	14%
A year	31%
Eighteen months	11%
Two years	13%
Three or four years	3%
Five years or more	1%
Don't know	23%

People thought many traditions were worth keeping but they felt strongly against others. **75%** thought that the bride's family paying for the wedding was a tradition that should be dropped.

Similarly **70%** of people thought that the tradition of the bride obeying her husband should be dropped.

Please say whether you think these wedding traditions are good ideas that should be preserved

(*Net scores)

Tradition	Net score
Groom having a best man	83%
Getting engaged before marriage	77%
Bride/groom taking first dance at reception	76%
Father giving bride away	73%
Bride throwing bouquet at end of reception	70%
Best man's speech	69%
Bride/groom not seeing each other on the morning of the wedding	53%
Bride taking husband's name	44%
Bride wearing white	27%
Proposing on bended knee	19%
Groom asking permission from bride's father	17%

*The net score is reached by subtracting the % who thought the tradition should be dropped from the % who thought it should be kept.

Some issues

• Why do you think some traditions are more important to people than others?

• Which traditions do you think are worth keeping and why?

• Do you expect these traditions to change in the future?

Financial issues

Managing money

A survey of 2,016 members of the GB public aged 16-75 revealed how much British households were feeling the pinch.

Figures may not add up to 100% due to rounding.

Sources and weblinks:
Source: Halifax Money Matters Survey;
Ipsos MORI/ Halifax
www.ipsos-mori.com

Three-quarters of Britons say they are coping well financially but over half are worried about bills

Which one of these best describes how well or badly your household is coping financially these days?

- Very well/ fairly well
- Fairly badly/ very badly
- Don't know

75%   23%   3%

How much do the following statements apply to you personally?

- Strongly/tend to agree
- Neither agree nor disagree
- Tend to disagree/ strongly disagree
- Don't know

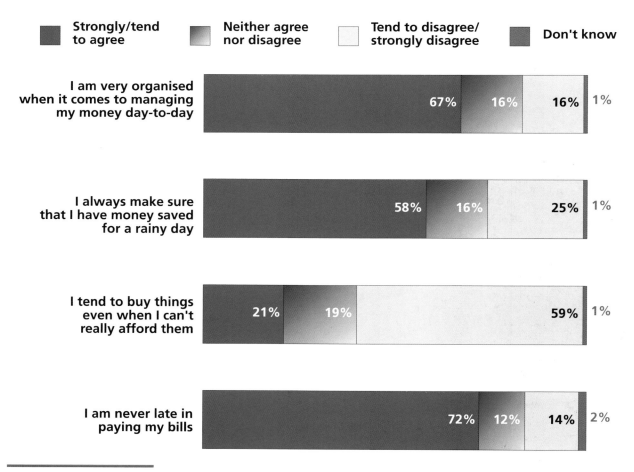

I am very organised when it comes to managing my money day-to-day — 67%   16%   16%   1%

I always make sure that I have money saved for a rainy day — 58%   16%   25%   1%

I tend to buy things even when I can't really afford them — 21%   19%   59%   1%

I am never late in paying my bills — 72%   12%   14%   2%

Better or worse off?

49% said they were **a little** or **a lot worse off** financially than this time last year.

Those in their 40s and 50s were the age groups most likely to rate their households as worse off financially compared to a year ago.

Savings

63% had dipped into savings to pay for something **essential**, at least once in the past 12 months.

Running out of money

46% said that their households had run out of money by the end of the month at least once in the past 12 months – this included **9%** who said they had run out **every** month.

Tipping point

People were asked how much living costs would have to increase to tip them over into difficulty. **13%** said this extra amount was **£24** or less. **46%** said it was **£99** or less.

Thinking about the next 12 months – percentages who were very or fairly concerned about their household's...

...ability to pay their rent/their mortgage repayments

32%

...ability to save money for the future

62%

...ability to pay off debts (eg credit cards or loans)

36%

...and their household having enough income to cover living costs and bills

53%

15% thought their financial situation would get **a little** or **a lot better** in the next 12 months.

40% thought it would **stay the same** and

40% thought it would get **a little** or **a lot worse**.

Some issues

- Most people seem to think they are well organised and careful with money. What can be done for those who aren't?

- If most people are good at managing money, why have almost half of households run out by the end of the month?

- Many people are worried about not having savings. Are they right to worry?

Trust in banks

People do not trust banks and want more information about how they are run

For the Public Trust in Banking report, YouGov spoke with twenty leading banking professionals and conducted three surveys with nationally representative samples of UK adults, totalling 11,089 individuals.

Sources and weblinks:
Source: YouGov Trust In Banking Report, 2013
www.yougov.co.uk

48% of people think the banking industry is holding the country back.

Many people feel negatively about banking and bankers without knowing a great deal about the issue. For this reason YouGov conducted two strands of research:

SURVEY 1: didn't provide any information but asked a number of broad questions about banks.

SURVEY 2: described a number of reforms that have taken place in recent years to clean up British banking. They also invited people to think about the importance of banking to Britain's economy.

They then repeated the broad questions that were asked in survey 1.

The results can be seen here: % who agree

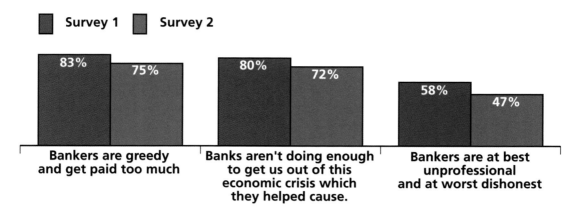

■ Survey 1   ■ Survey 2

	Survey 1	Survey 2
Bankers are greedy and get paid too much	83%	75%
Banks aren't doing enough to get us out of this economic crisis which they helped cause.	80%	72%
Bankers are at best unprofessional and at worst dishonest	58%	47%

> Even though more information meant people had a little more trust in banks, they still had doubts. People feel in the dark about the industry that controls so much of their money and they want it to improve. It is clear that more information is needed about how banking works.

Which of the following actions, if any, do you feel might be important in improving some of the problems associated with UK banking?

Select any that apply

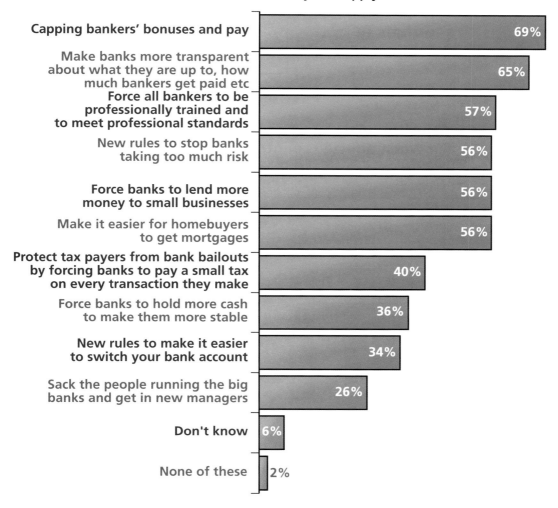

Capping bankers' bonuses and pay	69%
Make banks more transparent about what they are up to, how much bankers get paid etc	65%
Force all bankers to be professionally trained and to meet professional standards	57%
New rules to stop banks taking too much risk	56%
Force banks to lend more money to small businesses	56%
Make it easier for homebuyers to get mortgages	56%
Protect tax payers from bank bailouts by forcing banks to pay a small tax on every transaction they make	40%
Force banks to hold more cash to make them more stable	36%
New rules to make it easier to switch your bank account	34%
Sack the people running the big banks and get in new managers	26%
Don't know	6%
None of these	2%

Some issues

- Why do you think people care about bankers' bonuses?

- Do you think banks provide enough information about the way they work? And if so, is it easy to understand?

- What do you think banks should do to help people?

See also Essential Articles 2014, What irritates me about bankers, p92

Material deprivation

Across the EU there is a big difference in living conditions and some people have to do without basic resources in their everyday lives

The severe material deprivation rate measures the proportion of people **unable** to afford at least four of the following:

payment of mortgage/rent/bills/loans; adequate heating; unexpected financial expenses; eating meat or protein regularly; one week annual holiday; TV; washing machine; car; telephone.

Sources and weblinks:
Source: Poverty & Social Exclusion in the UK and EU 2005-2011,Office for National Statistics
© *Crown copyright 2013*
www.ons.gov.uk

Severe material deprivation % rates, by country, 2011
The ten worst affected countries and UK for comparison

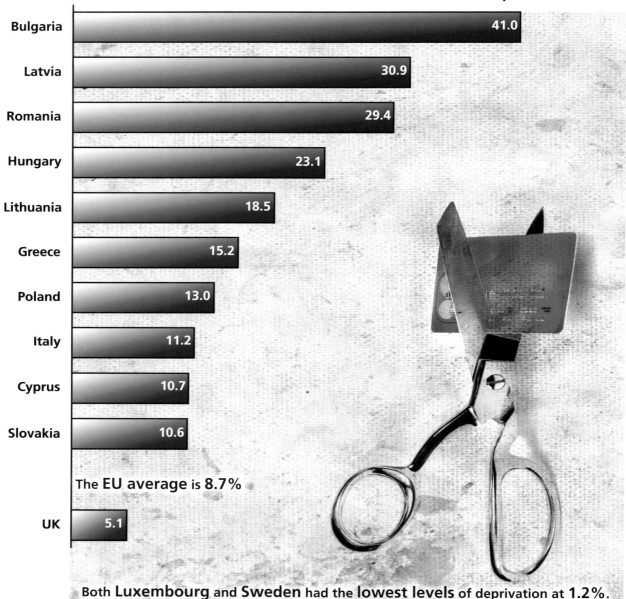

Country	Rate
Bulgaria	41.0
Latvia	30.9
Romania	29.4
Hungary	23.1
Lithuania	18.5
Greece	15.2
Poland	13.0
Italy	11.2
Cyprus	10.7
Slovakia	10.6
UK	5.1

The **EU average** is **8.7%**

Both **Luxembourg** and **Sweden** had the **lowest levels** of deprivation at **1.2%**.

Percentage of UK population UNABLE to afford selected items

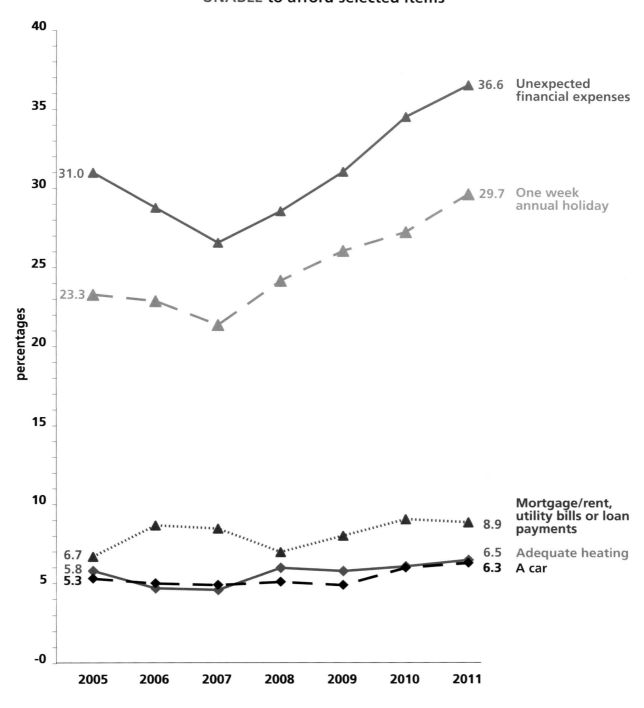

percentages

31.0 ... 36.6 Unexpected financial expenses

23.3 ... 29.7 One week annual holiday

Mortgage/rent, utility bills or loan payments

6.7
5.8
5.3
... 8.9
6.5 Adequate heating
6.3 A car

2005 2006 2007 2008 2009 2010 2011

In 2005, **6.1%** of people in the UK were unable to afford to eat meat or protein regularly, this decreased to **4.9%** in 2011.

The percentage of those unable to afford a TV, washing machine or telephone is consistently less than 1% and therefore not shown on the chart.

Some issues

- What do the deprivation levels suggest about the EU?

- Why do you think financial expenses and holidays feature so strongly on the UK chart?

- The trend in the case of mortgages etc is slightly different from the rest. What could be causing that difference?

Cost of a child

ICM research surveyed 1,000 parents of newborns to 11 year olds for The Halifax and used information from reports to find out the cost of raising a child.

Sources and weblinks:
Source: The Cost of Raising a Child, Halifax, 2013
www.halifax.co.uk
www.icm.org.uk

The average cost of raising a child to secondary school age now stands at almost £100,000

The average annual cost of raising a boy is £9,633.00 and £8,456.04 for a girl.

The total cost of raising a child from newborn to 11 is £105,963.00 for a boy and £93,016.44 for a girl!

Average monthly costs of raising a child by gender, £

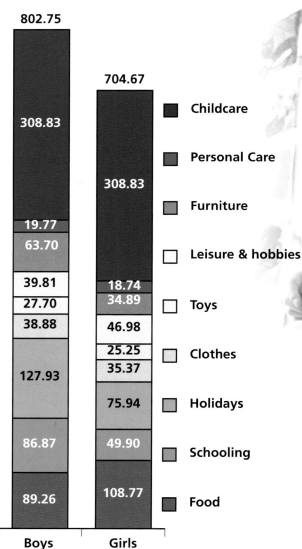

- 802.75
  - 308.83
  - 19.77
  - 63.70
  - 39.81
  - 27.70
  - 38.88
  - 127.93
  - 86.87
  - 89.26
- 704.67
  - 308.83
  - 18.74
  - 34.89
  - 46.98
  - 25.25
  - 35.37
  - 75.94
  - 49.90
  - 108.77

Boys | Girls

- ■ Childcare
- ■ Personal Care
- ■ Furniture
- ☐ Leisure & hobbies
- ☐ Toys
- ☐ Clothes
- ■ Holidays
- ■ Schooling
- ■ Food

On average £309 per month goes on child care. However, in London and the South East this costs £350; higher than anywhere else in the UK. Parents in the North West pay the least at £273 a month.

Children cost the most in the first year they are born (£11,573). This reduces with each phase of childhood, until the age of nine, where it increases again slightly to an average of £7,662.

Total costs by region
(newborn to age 11)

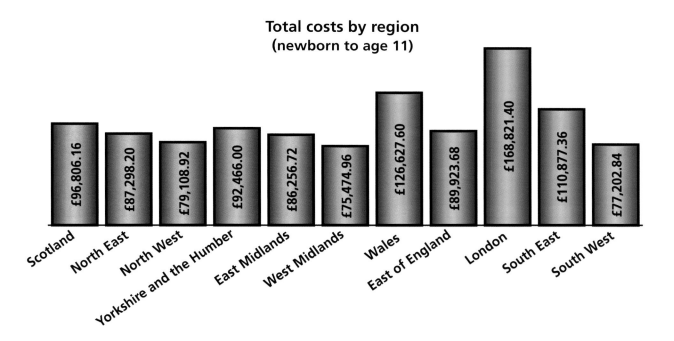

Region	Total cost
Scotland	£96,806.16
North East	£87,298.20
North West	£79,108.92
Yorkshire and the Humber	£92,466.00
East Midlands	£86,256.72
West Midlands	£75,474.96
Wales	£126,627.60
East of England	£89,923.68
London	£168,821.40
South East	£110,877.36
South West	£77,202.84

Parents in London pay most

They spend three and a half times as much a month on food for their children as those living in the North West, paying £239 compared to £68.

They also spend more than five times as much as parents in the West Midlands on holidays (£46 in the West Midlands compared to £242 in London).

Some issues

- Why do parents spend more on boys than girls?

- Why does it cost more to raise a child in London than in other areas?

- Childcare is the largest expense, can it be avoided or reduced?

Pocket money

Pocket money is at its highest since 2007

The Halifax Pocket Money report looks at how much money 8-15 year olds receive and their spending and saving habits. 1,296 children aged 8-15 were interviewed in June 2013 to find out about their pocket money.

Sources and weblinks:
Source: Annual Halifax Pocket Money Survey 2013
www.lloydsbankinggroup.com

Average pocket money

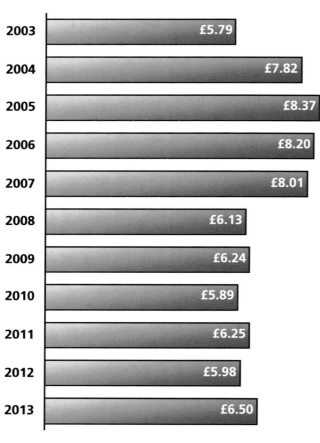

2003	£5.79
2004	£7.82
2005	£8.37
2006	£8.20
2007	£8.01
2008	£6.13
2009	£6.24
2010	£5.89
2011	£6.25
2012	£5.98
2013	£6.50

The number of children receiving weekly pocket money has increased, up 7% to 84% since 2012.

53% of children think that they get the right amount of pocket money.

75% save at least 25% of their pocket money.

42% keep their pocket money in a bank or building society account.

Some issues

- Do you think the economy might affect how much pocket money kids get?

- What do you think is the right amount of pocket money to receive?

- Do you think kids should have to 'work' or do tasks to get their spends?

Food & drink

Eating well

It is important to know what healthy eating is and give children a solid grounding in which to create healthy lives for themselves

Over 27,500 children across the UK were surveyed as part of the British Nutrition Foundation's Healthy Eating Week in 2013.

Sources and weblinks:
Source: British Nutrition Foundation
www.nutrition.org.uk

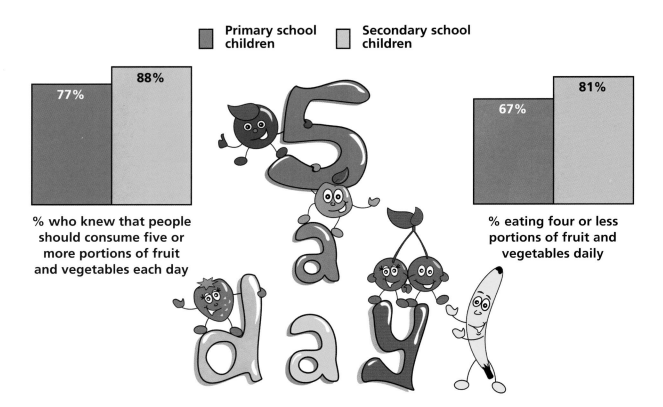

■ **Primary school children**   ■ **Secondary school children**

77%   88%

% who knew that people should consume five or more portions of fruit and vegetables each day

67%   81%

% eating four or less portions of fruit and vegetables daily

Where do foods come from?

29% of primary school children thought that cheese came from plants.

10% of secondary school children believed that tomatoes grow under the ground.

18% of primary school children said that fish fingers came from chicken.

40% of children at secondary school didn't think that frozen fruit and vegetables counted towards their five a day.

Breakfast

On the day of the survey *8%* of primary school children said they hadn't eaten breakfast that morning; this increased to *24%* in 11-14 year olds, then to *32%* of 14-16 year olds.

When asked if they usually had breakfast, *6%* of primary children and *19%* of 11-14 year olds and *25%* of 14-16 year olds said they didn't.

Fish

It is known that oily fish is good for health. National recommendations are that children and adults should consume *at least two portions* of fish each week.

16% of primary school children and *20%* of secondary school age said they *NEVER* ate fish.

Across all age groups from 5 to 16 year olds, only *17%* of children in the UK said they eat fish *twice a week.*

Healthy eating

This healthy plate shows how much of what you eat should come from each food group. It includes everything you eat during the day, including snacks.

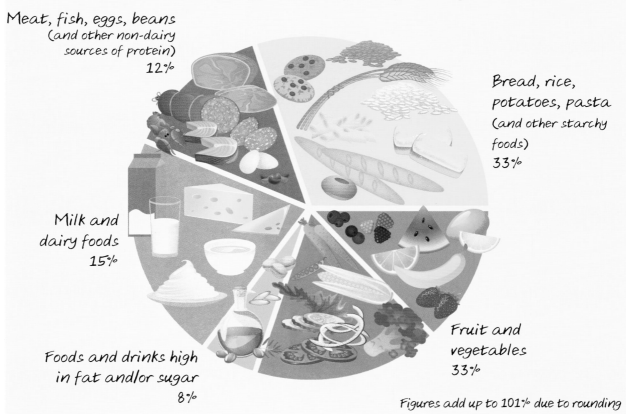

Meat, fish, eggs, beans
(and other non-dairy sources of protein)
12%

Bread, rice, potatoes, pasta
(and other starchy foods)
33%

Milk and dairy foods
15%

Fruit and vegetables
33%

Foods and drinks high in fat and/or sugar
8%

Figures add up to 101% due to rounding

Home cooking

17% of primary school children and *19%* of secondary school children cook at home either *every day* or *once a week*.

However *9%* of children at primary school and *11%* of children at secondary school *NEVER cook at home.*

84% of primary school children and *73%* of secondary school children *would like to cook more* and *85%* of children across all age groups say that they enjoy cooking.

Cost of food

The price of food is soaring, does this affect what we eat?

Each year, the government takes all the economic, social and environmental statistics about the food we eat and puts them into one 70-page "pocketbook". The results give us an insight into the nation's eating habits.

Sources and weblinks:
Source: Food Statistics Pocketbook 2013, DEFRA © Crown copyright 2013
www.defra.gov.uk

UK retail price changes by food group, 2007 to 2013,
(percentage increase in prices)

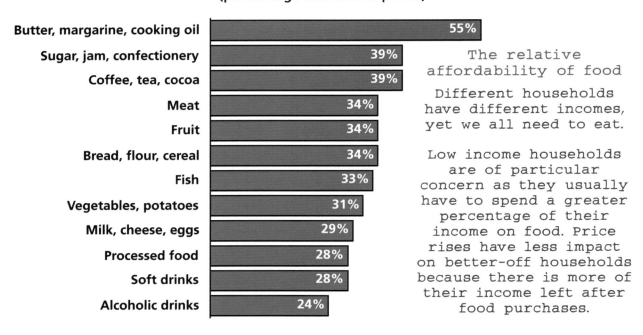

Food group	% increase
Butter, margarine, cooking oil	55%
Sugar, jam, confectionery	39%
Coffee, tea, cocoa	39%
Meat	34%
Fruit	34%
Bread, flour, cereal	34%
Fish	33%
Vegetables, potatoes	31%
Milk, cheese, eggs	29%
Processed food	28%
Soft drinks	28%
Alcoholic drinks	24%

The relative affordability of food

Different households have different incomes, yet we all need to eat.

Low income households are of particular concern as they usually have to spend a greater percentage of their income on food. Price rises have less impact on better-off households because there is more of their income left after food purchases.

How much in every £1 is spent on food?

The average UK household spends **11p** in every **£1** of income on food. However, in the poorest **20%** of households this rises to **17p**. This means proportionally, more of their income is spent on food.

Many people have coped with the price rises by buying cheaper products. Lower income households have not managed to cut their food spending, possibly as they were already buying the budget options.

What influences shoppers' choices?
(mentioned in top 5 by more than 45% of shoppers)

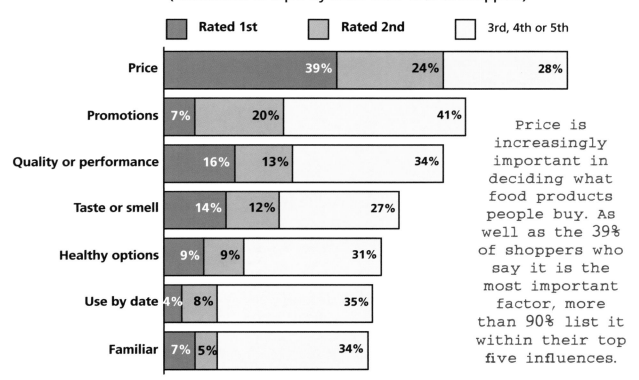

Rated 1st　　Rated 2nd　　3rd, 4th or 5th

	Rated 1st	Rated 2nd	3rd, 4th or 5th
Price	39%	24%	28%
Promotions	7%	20%	41%
Quality or performance	16%	13%	34%
Taste or smell	14%	12%	27%
Healthy options	9%	9%	31%
Use by date	4%	8%	35%
Familiar	7%	5%	34%

Price is increasingly important in deciding what food products people buy. As well as the 39% of shoppers who say it is the most important factor, more than 90% list it within their top five influences.

Affording your 5 a day

In the year to June 2013, fruit and vegetable prices showed the greatest increases at 7.5% and 5.2% respectively.

In fact between 2007 and 2011 the lowest income households bought 18% less of main cut meat, 15% less fruit, 12% less vegetables, 12% less fish and 12% less soft drinks.

Some issues

- Why do you think food prices are increasing?

- Why do you think some types of food increase in price more than others?

- If food is more expensive, how can people be encouraged to make healthy choices?

Organic market

Sales of organic food fell by 1.5% perhaps as a result of the economic downturn

The Soil Association Organic Market Report 2013 shows that although the economy is hitting organic sales, online spending is increasing, especially among younger consumers.

Sources and weblinks:
*Source: The Organic Market Report 2013,
The Soil Association*
www.soilassociation.org

Falling UK sales ... ...in supermarkets

£1.64 billion

2005   2008   2012

The seven leading supermarket chains saw their organic sales fall by **3.8%**.

BOX SCHEME & HOME DELIVERY SALES UP **4.4%**

THIS WAY UP

...but not elsewhere

The organic market may be affected on the high street, but it is booming online and in large specialist retailers.

Home delivery

Organic shoppers are increasingly choosing home delivery and specialist shops because they offer convenience and variety.

And online

Online purchases now amount to **10.1%** of spending on organic products through the major retailers compared to **5.7%** on all food and drink

ONLINE SALES **£4.1m** A WEEK

80.3% of households buy organic products.
55% of shoppers say they believe it is important to do so.
Only 6% think shopping organic is 'not at all important'.

Top reasons for buying organic

▶ main reason ▶ all reasons mentioned

Healthier for me and my family
25%   55%

Fewer chemicals
17%   53%

Natural and unprocessed
12%   52%

Better for nature/the environment
6%   44%

Safer to eat
7%   39%

Organic food tastes better
11%   35%

Organic farming is kinder to animals
10%   31%

More ethical
3%   29%

No GM ingredients
4%   28%

THE COMMITTED CORE
More than three-quarters of households buy organic products but sales are dominated by a small core of committed shoppers.

33% of organic shoppers account for **85%** of spending and just **6%** of shoppers are responsible for **51%** of all sales. The most committed buyers are aged 28-44.

Ethically aware under-35s increased their average spend

YOUNGER SHOPPERS LEAD THE WAY:

The 'Jamie Generation' of ethically aware under-35s (**16%** of sales) significantly increased their average spending in 2012.
The youngest organic shoppers (under-28s) are spending more on organic products than they did a year ago. Students are following suit. Their purchases increased by **15%** in 2012.

Middle-income Britain's share of organic spending has decreased

THE SQUEEZED MIDDLE

In the past year the proportion of spending by middle-income shoppers, has decreased from **34%** to **32%**.

This may be because this group face economic difficulties and are cutting back.

Share of organic sales within Great Britain

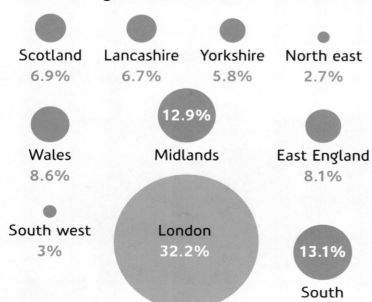

Scotland 6.9%

Lancashire 6.7%

Yorkshire 5.8%

North east 2.7%

Wales 8.6%

Midlands 12.9%

East England 8.1%

South west 3%

London 32.2%

South 13.1%

Some issues

- Do you think it is important for people to buy organic produce?

- Would you prefer to eat organic food?

- How do you think retailers can encourage more people to buy organic?

Health

State of health

There is a general pattern of better health in the South and worse health in the North

The 2011 Census included a question on general health and this information helps to assess the nation's health status and to make comparisons between areas within England and Wales.

Sources and weblinks:
Source: General Health in England and Wales 2011
© Crown copyright 2013
www.ons.gov.uk

How would you rate your general health over the last 12 months?

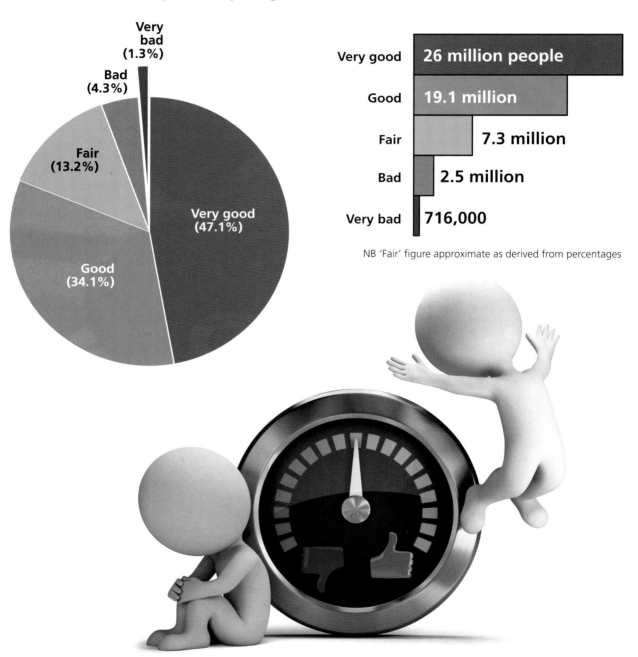

Very bad (1.3%)
Bad (4.3%)
Fair (13.2%)
Very good (47.1%)
Good (34.1%)

Very good — 26 million people
Good — 19.1 million
Fair — 7.3 million
Bad — 2.5 million
Very bad — 716,000

NB 'Fair' figure approximate as derived from percentages

Regional comparisons

- The general health profile of London's population was better than any other region. **50.5%** said their health was **very good**, **33.3%** said **good**. Only **5%** assessed their health as either **bad or very bad**. This is partly because London has a generally younger population.

- In the North East region and in Wales only **44%** said they had **very good** health while **7.4%** reported their health as **bad or very bad**.

- The average percentage for people in England reporting **good** health is **81.39%**. Areas with higher percentages include: London **83.84%**, the South East **83.65%**, the East of England **82.46%** and the South West **81.42%**.

- Areas with lower than average percentages of good health are: the North East **77.33%**, North West **79.28%** and Yorkshire & the Humber, **79.97%**.

The regions with the lowest percentage of people with good health in 2001 saw their rates fall further in 2011.
Those with a high percentage of good health in 2001 saw their rates rise.

Percentage change in good health between 2001 and 2011

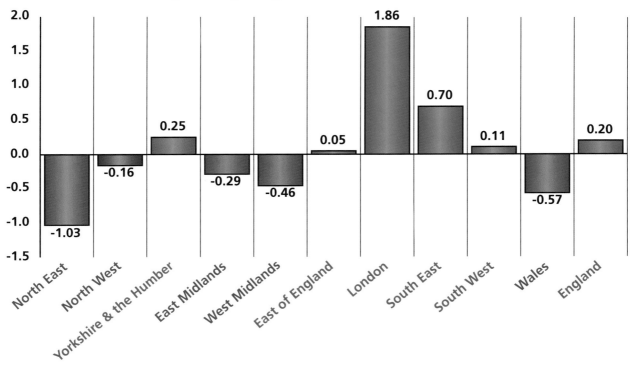

North East	-1.03
North West	-0.16
Yorkshire & the Humber	0.25
East Midlands	-0.29
West Midlands	-0.46
East of England	0.05
London	1.86
South East	0.70
South West	0.11
Wales	-0.57
England	0.20

Some issues

- What do you think defines very good health?

- Why would there be health differences in different regions of the country?

- Are there any other reasons you can think of for London having the greatest number of people in very good health?

Dementia

The term dementia describes a set of symptoms including memory loss, mood changes, and problems with communication and reasoning. The symptoms gradually get worse.

It is not a natural part of growing old. It is caused by diseases of the brain, the most common being Alzheimer's.

Sources and weblinks:
Source: Dementia 2013 – The hidden voice of loneliness © Alzheimer's Society 2013; Yougov
www.alzheimers.org.uk/dementia2013
www.yougov.co.uk

The number of people in the UK with dementia will double in the next 40 years

The size of the challenge

The breakdown of the population with dementia across the UK

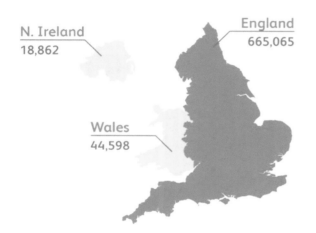

Scotland
approx
84,000

UK total
800,000

N. Ireland
18,862

England
665,065

Wales
44,598

Dementia is most common in older people but younger people (under 65) can get it too

40–64 years
1 in 1,400

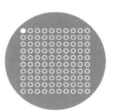

65–69 years
1 in 100

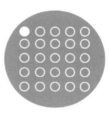

70–79 years
1 in 25

80+ years
1 in 6

Two thirds of people with dementia are women

- Only **44%** of people actually living with dementia have been diagnosed as having the disease.

- **61%** of people in England, Wales and Northern Ireland said they were living well with dementia – however, **17%** said they weren't.

- **33%** of people with dementia said they lost friends following a diagnosis.

- **62%** of people with dementia who lived on their own said they felt lonely. Difficulties in maintaining social relationships and other symptoms of dementia contributed to this.

- **39%** of people with dementia said they felt lonely compared to **24%** of those over 55 in the general public.

Future projections

 = 10,000 people

800,000 people
with dementia in
2012

1,000,000 people
with dementia in
2021

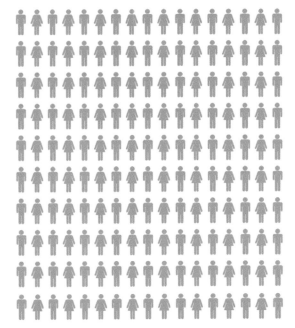

1,700,000 people
with dementia in
2051

Caring for someone with dementia is not an easy thing to do. You watch someone you love slowly lose the power to remember and the power to say and do things they once knew.

Arlene Phillips CBE, Alzheimer's Society Ambassador

Cost to society

Some of the cost of dementia is hidden by the work done by family carers supporting people at home

£23bn
**Cost of dementia
to the UK**

£8bn
Value to the
UK of the
work done by
family carers

Some issues

- Apart from the sufferers, who else might be affected by the increase in dementia?

- What economic effects might this have?

- How can people with dementia, and their families and friends, be supported?

See also Care & carers section, p41-52

Measles

Measles is a highly infectious viral illness. It can lead to serious complications, including blindness and even death.

Immunisation programmes provide protection to those who've been vaccinated and can also provide protection to the wider unvaccinated population. Where this happens, it is known as "herd immunity".

Cases of measles are at the highest level for 18 years

Sources and weblinks:

Source: Public Health England; NHS choices
www.hpa.org.uk
www.nhs.uk

Confirmed cases of measles, England and Wales, 1996-2012

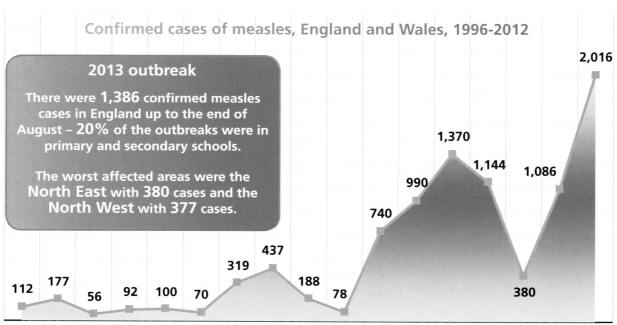

2013 outbreak

There were **1,386** confirmed measles cases in England up to the end of August – **20%** of the outbreaks were in primary and secondary schools.

The worst affected areas were the **North East** with **380** cases and the **North West** with **377** cases.

Year	Cases
1996	112
1997	177
1998	56
1999	92
2000	100
2001	70
2002	319
2003	437
2004	188
2005	78
2006	740
2007	990
2008	1,370
2009	1,144
2010	380
2011	1,086
2012	2,016

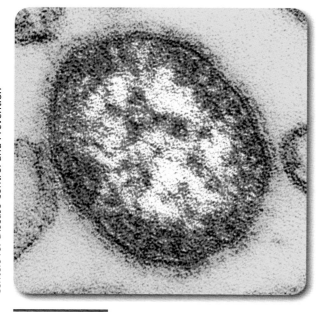

Photo: Particle of a measles virus
Centers for Disease Control and Prevention

The rise in measles cases is mostly due to the proportion of young people now aged 10-16 years who missed out on the MMR (measles, mumps & rubella) vaccination in the late 1990s and early 2000s.

Scare stories had linked the vaccination to autism and caused a drop in the number of parents taking their children to be vaccinated or taking them back for the second dose.

Two doses of the MMR vaccine, anytime from the age of 12 months up to the child's 5th birthday, are needed to achieve the greatest immunity and prevent any further outbreaks.

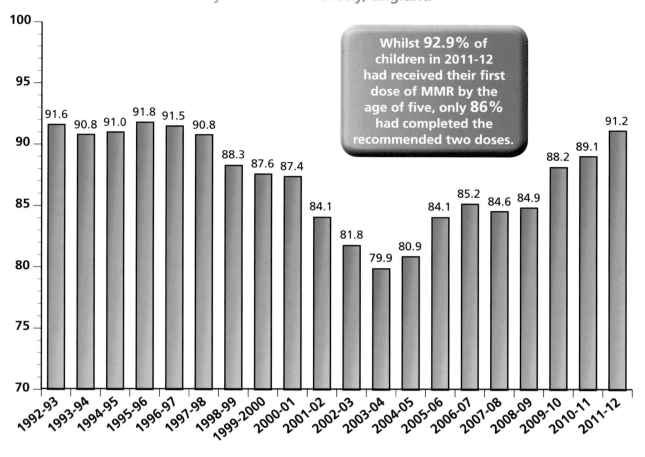

% of children immunised with **1st dose** of MMR vaccine by their 2nd birthday, England

Whilst **92.9%** of children in 2011-12 had received their first dose of MMR by the age of five, only **86%** had completed the recommended two doses.

Chart values:
- 1992-93: 91.6
- 1993-94: 90.8
- 1994-95: 91.0
- 1995-96: 91.8
- 1996-97: 91.5
- 1997-98: 90.8
- 1998-99: 88.3
- 1999-2000: 87.6
- 2000-01: 87.4
- 2001-02: 84.1
- 2002-03: 81.8
- 2003-04: 79.9
- 2004-05: 80.9
- 2005-06: 84.1
- 2006-07: 85.2
- 2007-08: 84.6
- 2008-09: 84.9
- 2009-10: 88.2
- 2010-11: 89.1
- 2011-12: 91.2

MMR uptake

In April 2013 a national catch-up programme to increase MMR uptake in children and teenagers was announced.

At that date, around a **third of a million** 10-16 year-olds were unvaccinated and another **third of a million** needed at least one further dose of MMR to give them full protection.

An additional **third of a million** children below and above this age band needed at least one further dose of MMR.

Some issues

- The untested research that linked measles vaccine to autism was widely reported. Were the newspapers wrong to spread this story?

- Do parents have a duty to have their children vaccinated against disease?

- Some schools considered banning students who hadn't been vaccinated and who didn't 'catch up'. Would that be a good decision?

Organ donation

Organ donations continue to rise, but there is a worry about the quality of organs

The UK Transplant Registry gives the figures behind organ donation.

The number of people on the transplant list has fallen because an increasing number of transplants are performed.

The number of patients joining the transplant list each year has stayed reasonably steady.

Sources and weblinks:
Source: Organ donation and transplant activity report 2012/2013
www.organdonation.nhs.uk

In 2012-13 there were 1,212 deceased donors. The lives of 4,212 patients were saved or improved by an organ transplant (a 6% increase on 2011-12).

The 1,212 deceased organ donors gave 4,096 organs. This represents a 10% increase in organs donated.

95% gave a kidney and 72% of these also donated at least one other organ.

There were also 1,101 living donors most of whom donated a kidney. 33 living donors donated part of a liver.

Number of deceased donors and transplants in the UK, 01/04/03 - 31/03/13, and patients on the active transplant list at 31 March

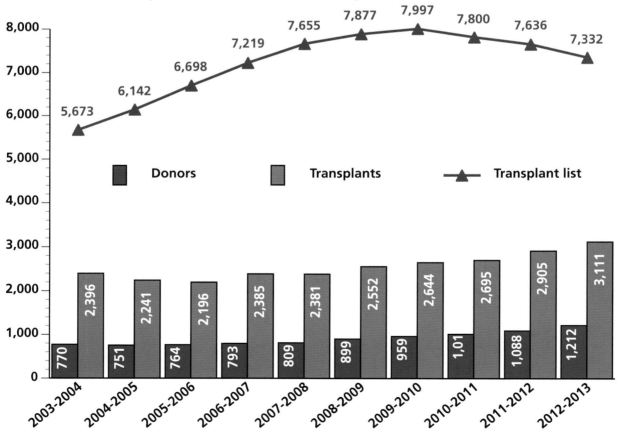

Transplant list values:
- 2003-2004: 5,673
- 2004-2005: 6,142
- 2005-2006: 6,698
- 2006-2007: 7,219
- 2007-2008: 7,655
- 2008-2009: 7,877
- 2009-2010: 7,997
- 2010-2011: 7,800
- 2011-2012: 7,636
- 2012-2013: 7,332

Year	Donors	Transplants
2003-2004	770	2,396
2004-2005	751	2,241
2005-2006	764	2,196
2006-2007	793	2,385
2007-2008	809	2,381
2008-2009	899	2,552
2009-2010	959	2,644
2010-2011	1,01	2,695
2011-2012	1,088	2,905
2012-2013	1,212	3,111

Legend: Donors · Transplants · Transplant list

The number of donors is increasing but the type of donor is changing. These changes could affect the quality of the organs donated and how well the transplant works for the person receiving it.

AGEING DONORS:
In 2012-2013, **34%** of deceased donors were aged 60 years or more compared with **16%** in 2003-2004. In particular the proportion of these donors aged at least 70 years has increased from **2%** to **12%** over the same time period.

OBESE DONORS:
The proportion of clinically obese donors, those with a Body Mass Index (BMI) of 30 or higher, has increased from **16%** to **26%** in deceased donors in the last 10 years.

BMI of deceased donors in the UK, 01/04/03 - 31/03/13
(donors for whom BMI was available)

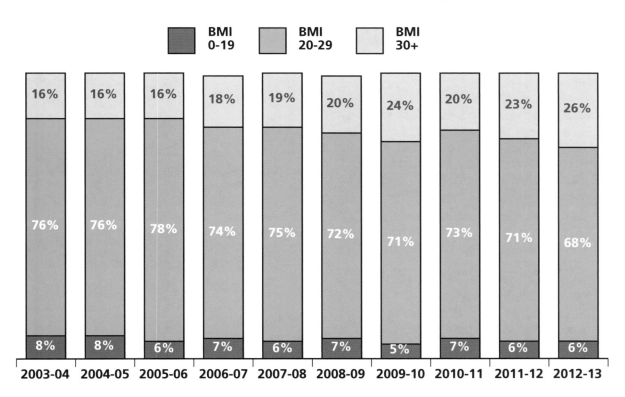

| | BMI 0-19 | BMI 20-29 | BMI 30+ |

Figures may not add up to 100% due to rounding

Some issues

- Why do you think the number of organ donors is increasing?

- What can be done to attract more donors?

- Why do you think there has been an increase in obese and older donors?

See also Increase in obesity p122

Eating disorders

More people than ever know about eating disorders through the media, but the images that go with the stories may be harmful and misleading

Over 1,000 people who had personal experience of an eating disorder were surveyed to find out how they felt about the way eating disorders were portrayed in the media.

Sources and weblinks:
Beat – beating eating disorders;
HES online Hospital Episode Statistics
www.b-eat.co.uk
www.hesonline.nhs.uk

beat Youthline 0845 634 7650

The facts:

Eating disorders can affect someone not only **physically** but can also affect their **mental state** and their **ability to interact with others**.

A person with an eating disorder may focus excessively on their weight, body shape and image. They may appear to have an **abnormal attitude towards food**, which will affect their behaviour and eating habits and can damage their health.

Of those interviewed by B-eat **66%** said media images had a negative impact on their self esteem, **70%** said it affected their body image

77% found the media too focused on weight and the physical symptoms of an eating disorder, not reporting on the mental distress and psychological root of the illness.

In their own words:

"...some magazines only run stories if they have pictures of peoples' 'lowest weights' – that needs to change, weight is just a symptom."

"...in order to recover and stay well I have had to distance myself from most media coverage"

"They always show pictures of a person at their worst which can be very triggering for sufferers"

"... It makes me want to compete with the person and become thinner than them... "

Number of hospital admissions for eating disorders 2011 to 2012

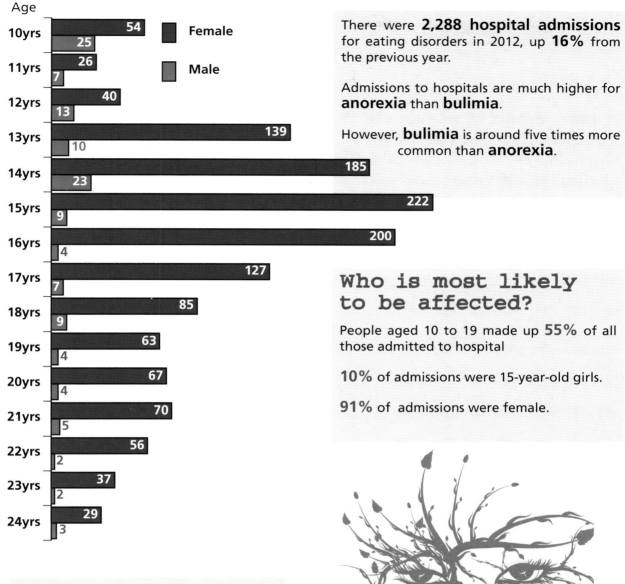

Age

	Female	Male
10yrs	54	25
11yrs	26	7
12yrs	40	13
13yrs	139	10
14yrs	185	23
15yrs	222	9
16yrs	200	4
17yrs	127	7
18yrs	85	9
19yrs	63	4
20yrs	67	4
21yrs	70	5
22yrs	56	2
23yrs	37	2
24yrs	29	3

There were **2,288 hospital admissions** for eating disorders in 2012, up **16%** from the previous year.

Admissions to hospitals are much higher for **anorexia** than **bulimia**.

However, **bulimia** is around five times more common than **anorexia**.

Who is most likely to be affected?

People aged 10 to 19 made up **55%** of all those admitted to hospital

10% of admissions were 15-year-old girls.

91% of admissions were female.

B-eat asked the general public:

Can you name an eating disorder?

72% said **anorexia**. Only **3%** said **binge eating**.

Yet **anorexia** is the **rarest** eating disorder, only **10%** of cases.

Can you tell if someone has an eating disorder?

Half said they could because the person would be very thin.

BUT most people with eating disorders won't be underweight at all. Over **80%** of people with an eating disorder are **overweight**.

Some issues

- Why do you think there are more hospital admissions for anorexia than for bulimia?
- Can you suggest any reasons for the rise in admissions in the teenage years?
- Why do you think the general public knows more about anorexia than bulimia?
- Is media coverage helpful or harmful?

See also Essential Articles 2014, I've seen the agony of anorexia, p116 and Eating disorders in Complete Issues

Increase in obesity

More adults than ever are overweight, but the biggest increase is in obesity – which brings health risks and costs

This annual statistical report presents a range of information on obesity drawn from a variety of previously published sources.

Sources and weblinks:
Source: Statistics on Obesity Physical Activity and Diet, England 2013, Health & Social Care Information Centre © Crown copyright 2013
www.hscic.gov.uk

The definition:

Body Mass Index (BMI) is measured by comparing weight to height.

A combination of weight, height and waist circumference is used to assess health risks from obesity in adults.

Normal BMI is 18.5 to less than 25, overweight is 25 to less than 30.

A person with a BMI of 30 or above and a waist measurement of more than 102cm for men or 88cm for women is at very high risk of health problems.

The size of the problem:

Between 1993 and 2011 the proportion of obese adults in **England** increased from **13%** to **24%** for men and from **16%** to **26%** for women.

The proportion of adults with a raised waist circumference increased from **20%** to **34%** among men and from **26%** to **47%** among women during the same period.

In **Scotland** in 2011 **27.7%** of adults were classified as obese. In Wales the figure was **22.1%**.

Relative risk factors for obese people of developing selected diseases

Obesity is a major public health problem because it increases the likelihood of people suffering serious chronic diseases.

The increased risks for obese people compared to the non-obese population are shown in the table on the right.

For example, an obese woman is nearly 13 times more likely to develop type 2 diabetes than a woman who is not obese.

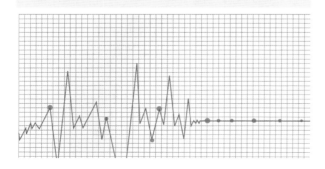

How much more likely an obese person is to suffer from:	Men	Women
Type 2 diabetes	5.2	12.7
High blood pressure	2.6	4.2
Heart attack	1.5	3.2
Cancer of the colon	3.0	2.7
Angina	1.8	1.8
Gall bladder diseases	1.8	1.8
Ovarian cancer	-	1.7
Osteoarthritis	1.9	1.4
Stroke	1.3	1.3

Estimates for England from the National Audit Office

Number of hospital admissions where obesity was the primary (main) or secondary reason

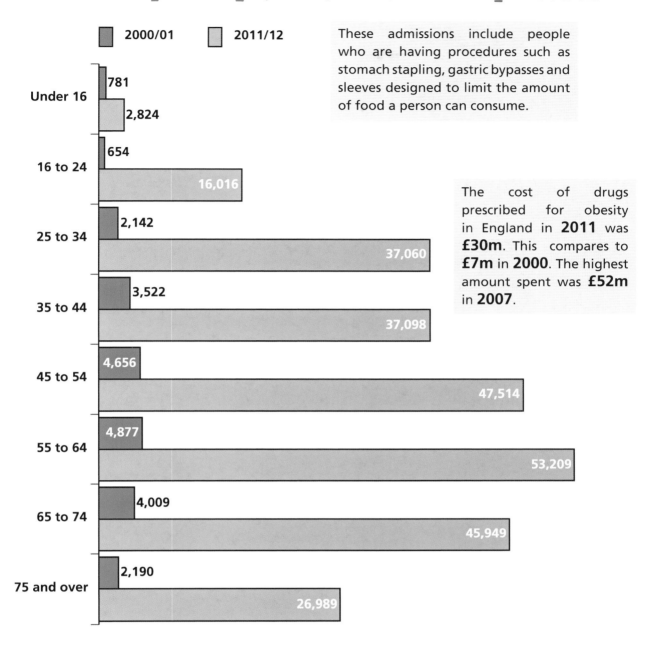

2000/01 **2011/12**

Under 16
781
2,824

16 to 24
654
16,016

25 to 34
2,142
37,060

35 to 44
3,522
37,098

45 to 54
4,656
47,514

55 to 64
4,877
53,209

65 to 74
4,009
45,949

75 and over
2,190
26,989

These admissions include people who are having procedures such as stomach stapling, gastric bypasses and sleeves designed to limit the amount of food a person can consume.

The cost of drugs prescribed for obesity in England in **2011** was **£30m**. This compares to **£7m** in **2000**. The highest amount spent was **£52m** in **2007**.

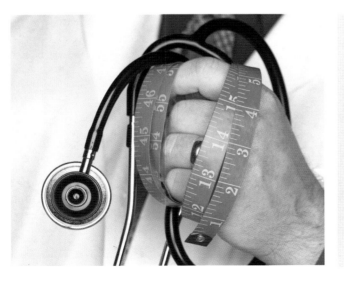

Some issues

- Why do you think there are more hospital admissions for obesity than before?
- How concerned should we be about this?
- What would help to control the 'obesity epidemic'?
- Is media coverage helpful or harmful?

See also Essential Articles 2014, It's time to think big to tackle obesity crisis, p124 and Debate: Is it wrong for employers to discriminate against obese people? p198

Wrong weight

Parents and children are not always good at judging what is a healthy weight

The Health Survey for England (HSE) is part of a programme of surveys commissioned by the Health and Social Care Information Centre to provide regular information concerning the public's health.

A total of **8,610** adults and **2,007** children were interviewed for this survey, part of which focused on weight.

NB Figures do not add up to 100% due to rounding

Sources and weblinks:
*Source: Health Survey for England
Health & Social Care Information Centre
© Crown copyright 2013
www.hscic.gov.uk*

To live a healthy life people need to be able to judge whether their own weight is healthy.

This study showed that people overestimated their height and underestimated their weight - and that of their children.

Parents and children

Actual status of children whose parents thought they were at the right weight

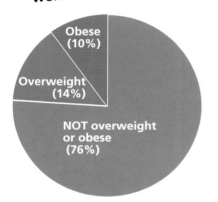

- Obese (10%)
- Overweight (14%)
- NOT overweight or obese (76%)

78% of parents thought their child was about the **right weight**. When **children** were asked about their weight **60%** of boys and **53%** of girls put themselves in the **'right weight'** category. However, in both cases, a proportion of the children were overweight or obese.

Actual status of children who thought they were at the right weight

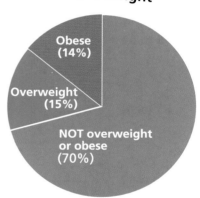

- Obese (14%)
- Overweight (15%)
- NOT overweight or obese (70%)

Among the parents of **obese** children **47%** judged their child's weight to be about right and **84%** of parents with **overweight** children also thought their child was at the right weight.

Some issues

- Why does it matter that people misjudge weight?

- Why is it particularly important for children not to be overweight?

- What would cause parents to think their children were at the correct weight even if they were obese?

See also Increase in obesity p122

Internet
& media

Safer internet

Young people's attitudes towards online rights and responsibilities

11,757 primary and 12,340 secondary children from the UK took part in the 'Have your Say' survey.

They were asked to vote on the online rights and responsibilities they thought were most important to them.

Sources and weblinks:

Source: 'Have your Say' survey, UK Safer Internet Centre
www.saferinternet.org.uk

■ **Primary (aged 7-11)**　■ **Secondary (aged 11-19)**

The right to feel safe

% of young people who believe they have the right to feel safe online

Feeling safe was selected as the **most important** right by both age groups.

57%　63%

Young people recognise they have a responsibility to help others stay safe online too

% who would tell a friend if something upset or worried them online

53%

32%

% who would turn to an older brother or sister for support

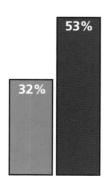

30%　27%

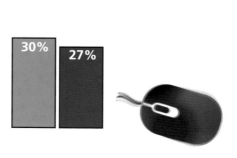

Parents play a key supporting role

% who turn to their parents or carer if something upsets or worries them online

79%

66%

Young people of all ages are enjoying the benefits of the internet:

- a wide range of content;

- connecting with their friends and family;

- the potential to create and distribute their own content.

BUT there are some things that **stop them enjoying their online time** such as seeing things that upset or embarrassed them.

34% of all children had seen something unpleasant or hurtful in the last year, eg scary videos, pictures and chainmail, violent films or games, or 'rude' things and swearing.

What stops young people enjoying their time online?

☐ **Primary (aged 7-11)**   ■ **Secondary (aged 11-19)**

% who said people being unkind (eg mean comments and behaviour)

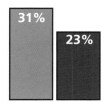

31%
23%

% who said adverts

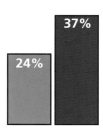

37%
24%

Young people said adverts, pop-ups in particular, were annoying, inappropriate and scary. Some worried they might get a virus by clicking on the advert.

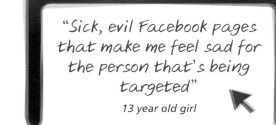

"Adverts that appear on harmless websites that are not appropriate"

12 year old boy

"Sick, evil Facebook pages that make me feel sad for the person that's being targeted"

13 year old girl

E-safety education

The right to be educated about staying safe online was voted in the top 10 rights on both the primary and secondary surveys.

80% of 7-19 year olds said they have been taught about staying safe online in the last year.

Some issues

- Are your concerns the same as those shown here?

- Should 7 year olds really be going online or are they too young?

- How could young people be protected against upset and abuse while also being able to benefit from the internet?

See also Internet trolls p128 and Internet slang p130

Internet trolls

A study suggests trolling is now more prevalent than real-life bullying

An online survey of 2,001 respondents aged 13 to 19 showed that teens are suffering online abuse in silence as most are not reporting it.

Sources and weblinks:

Source: Trolled Nation study by Knowthenet, January 2013
www.Knowthenet.org.uk

THE VICTIM...

75%

18 YEAR OLD GIRLS
say they have experienced online bullying or trolling

85%

19 YEAR OLD BOYS
have experienced online bullying or trolling

2/3 TEENAGERS
have experienced or know someone who has been affected by online bullying or trolling

TROLLING HOTSPOTS

The most popular sites and services for online trolling or bullying

87%	19%	13%	9%	8%	4%
FACEBOOK	**TWITTER**	**BBM** (BlackBerry Messenger)	**ASK.FM**	**BEBO**	**WHATSAPP**

SUFFERING IN SILENCE

Over a third of those surveyed decided not to report the incident because they felt like no action would be taken

60% said they had **NEVER REPORTED THE PROBLEM TO THE WEBSITE**

22% of those who did in fact report it said **NOTHING HAD HAPPENED**

FEWER THAN 1 IN 5 (17%) of teens likely to **TELL A PARENT** they've been affected

ONLY 1% of teenagers say **TELLING A TEACHER** would be their first response to online bullying

WHAT ACTION SHOULD BE TAKEN?

Teens call for tougher action to deal with online trolls

64%
believe that not enough is currently being done by social networks to try to tackle the issue

53%
think that trolls should be banned from social media sites

42%
say that the experience would lead them to consider giving up their social networking site

TOP TIPS FOR TEENS

DON'T FEED THE TROLLS

Trolls feed off your response so whatever you do, never reply

TELL SOMEONE YOU TRUST

Tell a mate, a teacher, a parent, or someone you can trust about it as soon as possible

COLLECT EVIDENCE

Collect evidence of email or message trails in case it gets more serious. For a check list of what to save visit:
www.Knowthenet.org.uk/trolling

Some issues

- Why is internet bullying a particular problem for young people?

- Why do so few people report the problem?

- Why do people feel it is ok to be nasty?

- What action should victims, parents and others take?

See also Safer internet p126 and Internet slang p130

Internet slang

Parents and teenagers aren't on the same wavelength when it comes to how we communicate online

Knowthenet's UK survey of 1,001 parents with children aged 10 to 18 and an online survey of 1,013 teenagers aged 10 to 18 explored how much parents knew about common internet terms.

Sources and weblinks:
Source: Knowthenet
www.Knowthenet.org.uk

KNOWLEDGE GAP

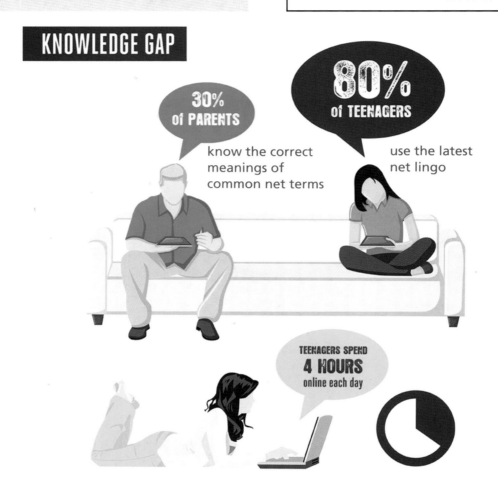

30% of PARENTS know the correct meanings of common net terms

80% of TEENAGERS use the latest net lingo

TEENAGERS SPEND **4 HOURS** online each day

PARENTS IN THE DARK?

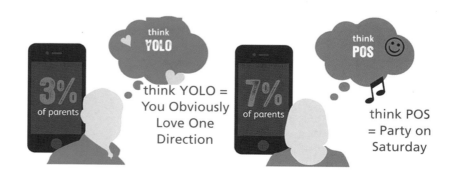

3% of parents think YOLO = You Obviously Love One Direction

7% of parents think POS = Party on Saturday

TRANSLATING NETSPEAK TERMS

Understanding what these key terms mean is vital in getting early warning if young people are involved in risky business online. Parents had low pass rates on key terms assessed in the survey:

LMIRL — 8% pass rate

Definition: Let's meet in real life

Parents may be unaware of teens planning to meet up with strangers they've chatted to online

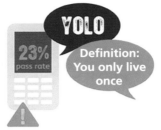

YOLO — 23% pass rate

Definition: You only live once

Parents may be unaware of their kids casually referencing dangerous scenarios they plan to get involved with

ASL — 27% pass rate

Definition: Age, Sex, Location

Parents may be unaware that their children are being asked for personal information

POS — 28% pass rate

Definition: Parents over shoulder

Parents might miss that their children are deliberately keeping information from them

TORRENTING — 35% parental concern

Definition: Transferring files illegally via websites

Parents can be unaware that their children are downloading illegal content. 32% of children admit to doing this

TROLLING — 58% pass rate

Definition: Repeatedly posting offensive remarks online to provoke a response

Parents may be unaware that their kids are being bullied online

Mums were a little more clued up than dads with **32%** correctly defining terms compared with **29%** of dads.

The survey also revealed that a large proportion of 10-18 year olds misbehave online, **30%** confessing to posting on friends' social network profiles without permission and **20%** saying they had been mean to others online.

Some issues

- Why should parents worry about not understanding some of these terms?

- Why would young people prefer to have some terms that parents don't understand?

- If someone you knew was taking risks online, what would you do?

See also Safer internet p126 and Internet trolls p128

Keeping in touch

The Ofcom report compares data on services and use in the UK and 16 other countries. Consumer research was conducted online with **9,152** people in nine countries including the UK.

Sources and weblinks:
Source: Ofcom International Communications Market Report, December 2012
www.ofcom.org.uk

Although most people would prefer face to face communication, we generally use other methods

How often do you use these methods to communicate with friends and family? UK

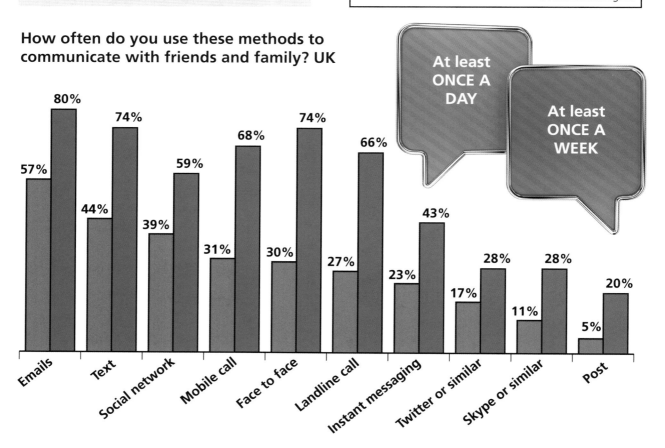

At least ONCE A DAY

At least ONCE A WEEK

The highest **daily** overall score was use of email by **65%** in Japan.

The highest overall **weekly** score was also email, used by **86%** in France.

When asked to pick **one** method of communicating with friends and family, the majority in the UK, **48%**, preferred **face to face** contact.

12% preferred **landline** calls; **12% email**; **7% mobile** calls; **7% text**; **5% social networks**; **3% Skype**; **2% instant messaging.** Others mentioned post, microblogging (Twitter), e-cards and picture messaging.

Some issues

- Why is there a difference between the way we would like to communicate and what we actually do?

- Do you think methods of communication will change in the future?

- Does technology help us communicate more or get in the way of proper personal relationships?

Language

Worst at languages

Most English students are not getting beyond a basic level in a foreign language, unlike other European countries

The European Survey on Language Competences (ESLC) was a survey of foreign language proficiency organised by the European Commission. A total of fourteen European countries participated in the survey.

In England the base was a random sample of those pupils who have chosen to continue learning a language in Key Stage 4.

Sources and weblinks:
Source: European Survey on Language Competence
www.nfer.ac.uk

Percentage of Independent, Basic and Less than basic foreign language users
(Tests of reading, listening and writing in the main language studied)

◻ Independent   ◼ Basic   ◻ Less than basic

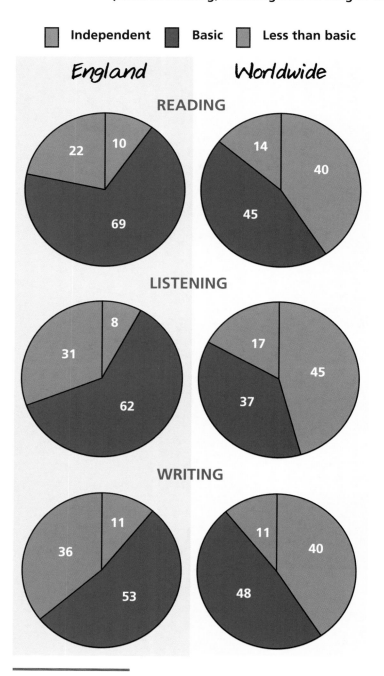

England / Worldwide

READING — England: 10, 22, 69 | Worldwide: 14, 40, 45

LISTENING — England: 8, 31, 62 | Worldwide: 17, 45, 37

WRITING — England: 11, 36, 53 | Worldwide: 11, 40, 48

Independent means: Being able to use language to read, understand or write the main points of an argument or text; ranging up to being able to deal with more complex texts and arguments and a greater variety of language. Higher level GCSE to A Level standard.

Basic means: Ranging from understanding or using a single word at a time or being able to pick up familiar words and phrases to being able to use short simple sentences from familiar situations. Entry level to Foundation GCSE.

LEARNING

ENGLISH · DEUTSCH · FRANÇAIS · ITALIANO · ESPAÑOL

NB % may not add up due to rounding

How much pupils like learning a language

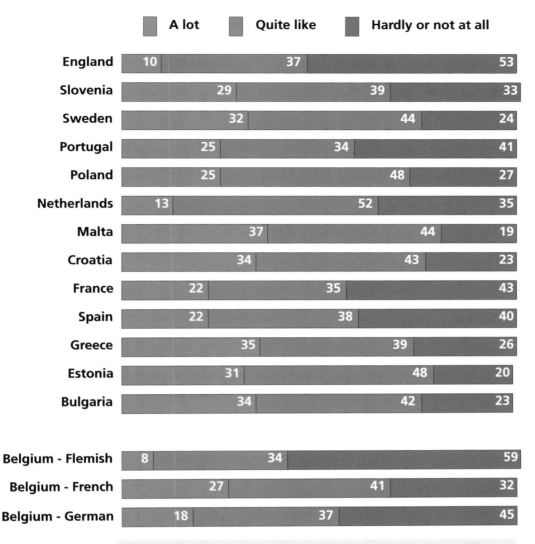

	A lot	Quite like	Hardly or not at all

Country	A lot	Quite like	Hardly or not at all
England	10	37	53
Slovenia	29	39	33
Sweden	32	44	24
Portugal	25	34	41
Poland	25	48	27
Netherlands	13	52	35
Malta	37	44	19
Croatia	34	43	23
France	22	35	43
Spain	22	38	40
Greece	35	39	26
Estonia	31	48	20
Bulgaria	34	42	23
Belgium - Flemish	8	34	59
Belgium - French	27	41	32
Belgium - German	18	37	45

14 countries were included but since Belgium has three language groups there were 16 sets of results. For 13 out of 16 the tests were in English. For England and for the Flemish and German speaking communities of Belgium the pupils were tested in French.

Some issues

- The speaking element has been left out of these tests. How important do you think this is?

- Why are other countries more successful at learning languages?

- Does liking a subject help you learn it?

- How could we improve our attitude to languages and our ability to learn?

See also Europeans and their languages p136

Europeans and their languages

Most Europeans have a very positive attitude towards mastering a foreign language

26,751 Europeans from 27 EU countries including the UK, were surveyed in 2012 to ask about their attitudes and behaviour towards languages.

88% of Europeans thought that knowing languages other than their own was very useful and 98% thought mastering foreign languages was useful for the future of their children.

Sources and weblinks:

Source: Europeans and their languages, Eurobarometer survey, TNS Opinion & Social network for European Commission
http://ec.europa.eu

Usefulness of language

When asked to name two languages they believed were most useful, firstly for **their own personal development:**

67% of Europeans surveyed said **English,** followed by **German, 17%**

and secondly, **for their children's future:**

79% said **English,** followed by both **French** and **German, 20%.**

Those surveyed were asked how many languages, other than their own mother tongue, they were able to speak well enough to HOLD A CONVERSATION

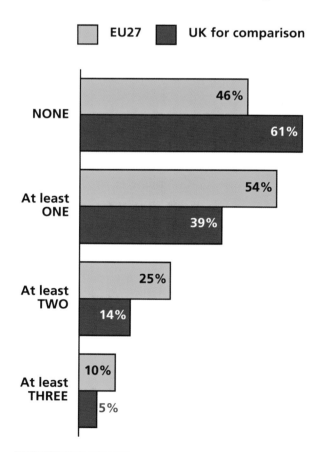

- EU27
- UK for comparison

NONE
- 46%
- 61%

At least ONE
- 54%
- 39%

At least TWO
- 25%
- 14%

At least THREE
- 10%
- 5%

Those surveyed were given a list of advantages of learning a new language and asked what they felt the main advantages were

(respondents could give more than one answer)

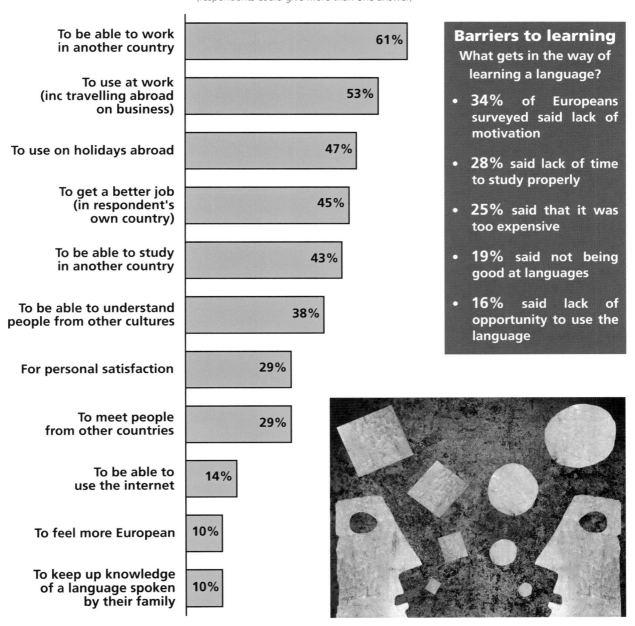

To be able to work in another country	61%
To use at work (inc travelling abroad on business)	53%
To use on holidays abroad	47%
To get a better job (in respondent's own country)	45%
To be able to study in another country	43%
To be able to understand people from other cultures	38%
For personal satisfaction	29%
To meet people from other countries	29%
To be able to use the internet	14%
To feel more European	10%
To keep up knowledge of a language spoken by their family	10%

Barriers to learning
What gets in the way of learning a language?

- **34%** of Europeans surveyed said lack of motivation

- **28%** said lack of time to study properly

- **25%** said that it was too expensive

- **19%** said not being good at languages

- **16%** said lack of opportunity to use the language

Speaking a language

84% of Europeans surveyed thought that everyone in the EU should speak one language in addition to their own and **72%** thought EU people should speak more than one foreign language.

Common language

69% of Europeans were in favour of people in the EU being able to speak a common language.

Some issues

- Are there reasons why the UK has fewer than average numbers able to speak another language?

- What do you think are the best reasons for learning another language?

- Do you think people would ever agree to have one common European language?

- Which language should that be and how could that language be chosen?

See also Worst at languages p134

Languages in England & Wales

More than 9 in every 10 people have English* as their main language

In March 2011 the Census showed that 92.3% of people aged three and over reported English* as their main language. Most of the people who have a different main language have English as a second language.

Sources and weblinks:
Source: Census 2011 – Office for National Statistics © Crown copyright 2013
www.ons.gov.uk

49.8 million people

said English* was their main language

The remaining 7.7% of the population – **4.2 million people** – had a main language other than English*

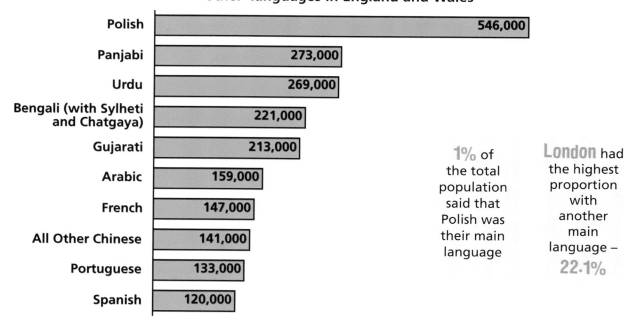

Number of people speaking the top ten main 'other' languages in England and Wales

Language	Number
Polish	546,000
Panjabi	273,000
Urdu	269,000
Bengali (with Sylheti and Chatgaya)	221,000
Gujarati	213,000
Arabic	159,000
French	147,000
All Other Chinese	141,000
Portuguese	133,000
Spanish	120,000

1% of the total population said that Polish was their main language

London had the highest proportion with another main language – **22.1%**

*English or Welsh in Wales
NB All Other Chinese is mixture of Chinese languages and excludes Mandarin Chinese and Cantonese Chinese

Concentration of languages across local authorities

Some 'Other' main languages were found to be concentrated in different local authorities eg **10,800** of those who reported Pakistani Pahari (with Mirpuri and Potwari) as their main language lived in Birmingham.

Highest percentage of 'other' language

Percentage of the population speaking English* as a main language

% (number of areas in brackets. Total =348)

	98.0 or over	(100)
	95.0 to 97.9	(124)
	86.0 to 94.9	(86)
	75.0 to 85.9	(26)
	under 75.0	(12)

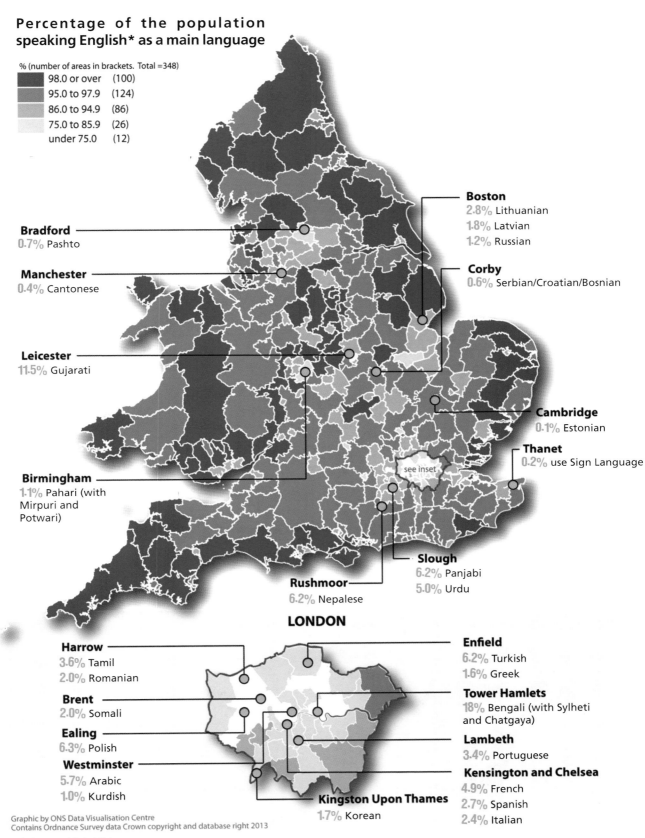

Bradford
0.7% Pashto

Manchester
0.4% Cantonese

Leicester
11.5% Gujarati

Birmingham
1.1% Pahari (with Mirpuri and Potwari)

Boston
2.8% Lithuanian
1.8% Latvian
1.2% Russian

Corby
0.6% Serbian/Croatian/Bosnian

Cambridge
0.1% Estonian

Thanet
0.2% use Sign Language

see inset

Slough
6.2% Panjabi
5.0% Urdu

Rushmoor
6.2% Nepalese

LONDON

Harrow
3.6% Tamil
2.0% Romanian

Brent
2.0% Somali

Ealing
6.3% Polish

Westminster
5.7% Arabic
1.0% Kurdish

Enfield
6.2% Turkish
1.6% Greek

Tower Hamlets
18% Bengali (with Sylheti and Chatgaya)

Lambeth
3.4% Portuguese

Kensington and Chelsea
4.9% French
2.7% Spanish
2.4% Italian

Kingston Upon Thames
1.7% Korean

Graphic by ONS Data Visualisation Centre
Contains Ordnance Survey data Crown copyright and database right 2013

*English or Welsh in Wales

Main language by English region and Wales, %

Legend: ■ English* □ Other

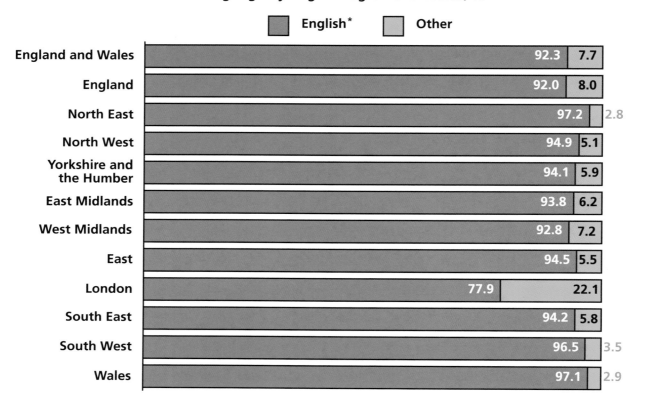

Region	English*	Other
England and Wales	92.3	7.7
England	92.0	8.0
North East	97.2	2.8
North West	94.9	5.1
Yorkshire and the Humber	94.1	5.9
East Midlands	93.8	6.2
West Midlands	92.8	7.2
East	94.5	5.5
London	77.9	22.1
South East	94.2	5.8
South West	96.5	3.5
Wales	97.1	2.9

How well do you speak English*?

Only 1.3% of the population **could not** speak English well.

0.3% reported that they **could not** speak English at all.

In London nearly 4.1% of the population were unable to speak English well or at all.

*English or Welsh in Wales

Welsh language

19% of people aged three and over in Wales were able to speak Welsh (562,000 people).

14.6% of the population in Wales were able to speak, read and write Welsh.

Nearly 75% of the population in Wales had no Welsh language skills.

Some issues

- Can you suggest why London has the highest proportion of non-native speakers?

- Can you draw any conclusions about the areas where 95% or more speak English or Welsh as a first language?

- How difficult is it for those people who cannot speak the language well or at all?

Sport & leisure

Olympic legacy

The Taking Part survey is based on adults and children living in private households in England. **9,838** people were interviewed for the 2012/13 survey.

_____

Sources and weblinks:
Source: Taking part survey and statistical releases, Department for Culture, Media and Sport © Crown copyright 2013
www.gov.uk

The public became more positive about the 2012 Olympic and Paralympic Games - but did they 'inspire a generation'?

Feelings about the UK hosting the Games

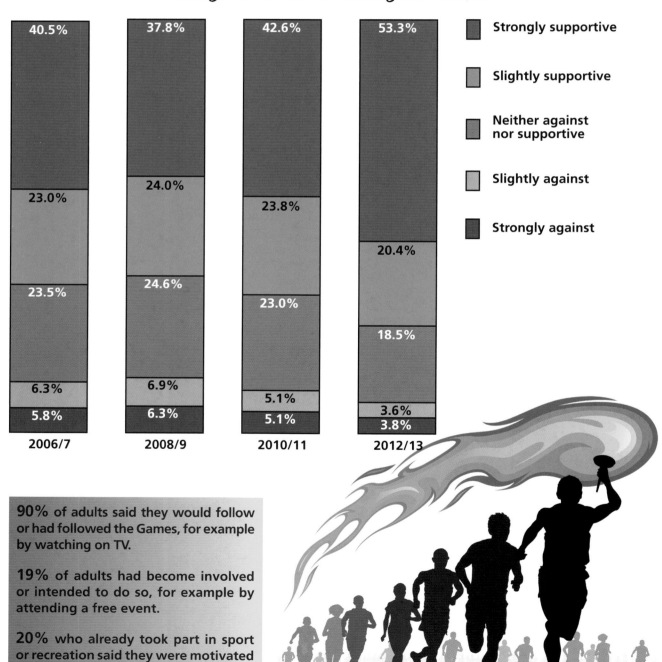

2006/7
- 40.5%
- 23.0%
- 23.5%
- 6.3%
- 5.8%

2008/9
- 37.8%
- 24.0%
- 24.6%
- 6.9%
- 6.3%

2010/11
- 42.6%
- 23.8%
- 23.0%
- 5.1%
- 5.1%

2012/13
- 53.3%
- 20.4%
- 18.5%
- 3.6%
- 3.8%

Legend:
- Strongly supportive
- Slightly supportive
- Neither against nor supportive
- Slightly against
- Strongly against

90% of adults said they would follow or had followed the Games, for example by watching on TV.

19% of adults had become involved or intended to do so, for example by attending a free event.

20% who already took part in sport or recreation said they were motivated to do more.

The children interviewed were asked:

"Would you say that the UK hosting the Olympics and Paralympics has encouraged you to take part in sport?"

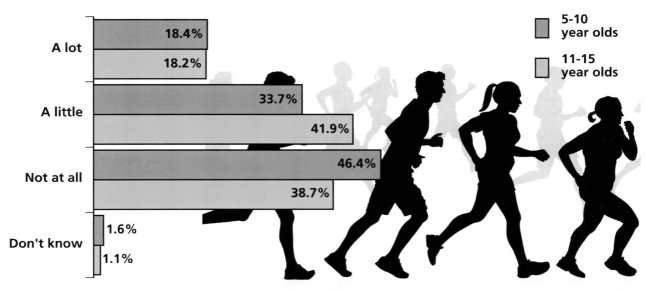

■	5-10 year olds
□	11-15 year olds

A lot
- 18.4%
- 18.2%

A little
- 33.7%
- 41.9%

Not at all
- 46.4%
- 38.7%

Don't know
- 1.6%
- 1.1%

Among those who were encouraged (either a little or a lot) to take part in sport:

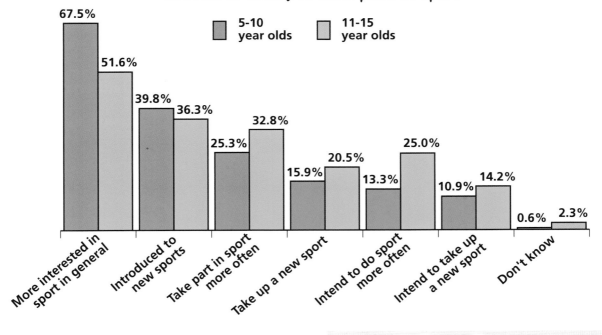

■	5-10 year olds
□	11-15 year olds

More interested in sport in general
- 67.5%
- 51.6%

Introduced to new sports
- 39.8%
- 36.3%

Take part in sport more often
- 25.3%
- 32.8%

Take up a new sport
- 15.9%
- 20.5%

Intend to do sport more often
- 13.3%
- 25.0%

Intend to take up a new sport
- 10.9%
- 14.2%

Don't know
- 0.6%
- 2.3%

Some issues

- When you look at the impact of the 2012 Games, which figure is more important - the percentage who were encouraged or the percentage who weren't?

- Should money for sport be spent on developing Olympic standard athletes or on sport for everyone?

- How can more young people be encouraged into sport?

Cheating at sport

Pressure to win can turn children into sports cheats

1,002 children aged 8-16 and a separate survey of **1,004 parents** of children aged 8-16 were asked for their opinions regarding sport and cheating.

NB figures may not add up to 100% due to rounding

Sources and weblinks:
Source: Marylebone Cricket Club and 'Chance to Shine' cricket charity
www.chancetoshine.org

The children were asked:

Q *Do you feel under pressure to win when you are playing sport?*

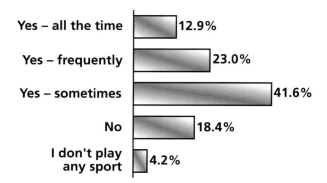

- Yes – all the time **12.9%**
- Yes – frequently **23.0%**
- Yes – sometimes **41.6%**
- No **18.4%**
- I don't play any sport **4.2%**

When **parents** were asked whether they thought their child felt under pressure to win, **67.2%** thought there was pressure and **25.4%** didn't think there was any at all.

This is different to what the **children** thought – **77.5%** felt under pressure to win.

75.9% of children thought that their teammates would cheat if they had the chance to get away with it

Q *Where does the pressure mostly come from?*

46.9% of children said **other children**, including **teammates**, **21.9%** said the pressure came from **themselves**.

Q *Do you think your teammates feel under pressure to win?*

90% of children said **yes**. **64.3%** thought that the pressure to win led their teammates to cheat.

77.3% of **parents** thought **they were** responsible for teaching children to play competitively but fairly.

6.8% of **parents** had never seen their child cheat.

59.1% of those **parents** who had seen their child cheat at sport felt **disappointed**.

49% of **parents** who had seen their child cheating had **confronted** him/her about it, but **44.2%** had **ignored** it.

64% of children in Britain's schools are cheating during school sport due to the pressure they feel under to win

The children were asked:

Q *How would you feel if the opposition cheated and got away with it?*

(more than one answer could be given)

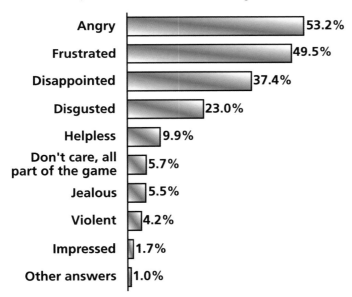

Angry	53.2%
Frustrated	49.5%
Disappointed	37.4%
Disgusted	23.0%
Helpless	9.9%
Don't care, all part of the game	5.7%
Jealous	5.5%
Violent	4.2%
Impressed	1.7%
Other answers	1.0%

Q *If your teammates win by cheating, how does it make them feel?*

37.1% thought they **didn't care**.

20.2% said their teammates **didn't cheat**.

18.9% said **winning** was the **most important** thing to them.

5.6% thought they'd feel **happy or proud**.

Only **16.4%** thought they would feel **guilty**.

64.9% of **parents** said that the cheating of some of today's high profile sportsmen and women added to the pressure on young people to copy them.

Some issues

- Are there any sports where winning isn't important?

- Do you agree that the attitudes of high-profile sports men and women affect young people?

- Are your sporting heroes people who try to win at all costs?

How active are children?

Only half of 7-year-old children in the UK achieve recommended levels of activity

A study of 6,497 children aged between 7 and 8 measured their levels of physical activity. They found that children were sedentary (inactive) for an average of 6.4 hours a day.

Sources and weblinks:
Source: How active are our children? Findings from the Millennium Cohort Study, BMJ Open 2013
www.bmjopen.bmj.com

The UK's chief medical officers recommend that one hour of exercise a day is the **minimum** needed to develop children's health and prevent them from becoming overweight or developing heart problems.

Percentage of children reaching recommended levels of activity

...by gender

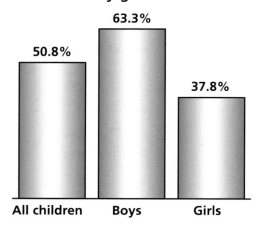

- All children: 50.8%
- Boys: 63.3%
- Girls: 37.8%

...by ethnicity

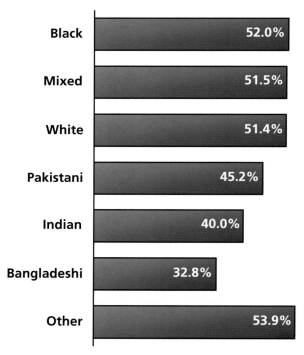

- Black: 52.0%
- Mixed: 51.5%
- White: 51.4%
- Pakistani: 45.2%
- Indian: 40.0%
- Bangladeshi: 32.8%
- Other: 53.9%

Children in Scotland were the most likely to be active with **52.5%** meeting the guidelines. In Wales the figure was **51.7%**, in England **50.9%** but in Northern Ireland only **43.4%** of children were active enough to protect their health.

Some issues

- Why are more boys active than girls?

- Why is a study of the activity of children important?

- Why is it important that children are more active?

- How can children be encouraged to be more active?

Active adults

How much time do you spend exercising each week?

The World Health Organization (WHO) recommends that 18-64 year olds should do **150 minutes** of **moderate** physical activity (eg gardening, dancing or brisk walking) or **75 minutes** of **vigorous** physical activity (eg playing sport, running or aerobics) per week.

A YouGov survey of 6,172 adults in five European countries compared results with the WHO recommendations to find out how active adults were.

Sources and weblinks:
Source: World Heart Federation
www.world-heart-federation.org

 In the last seven days, approximately how much time, if any, would you estimate you have spent doing...

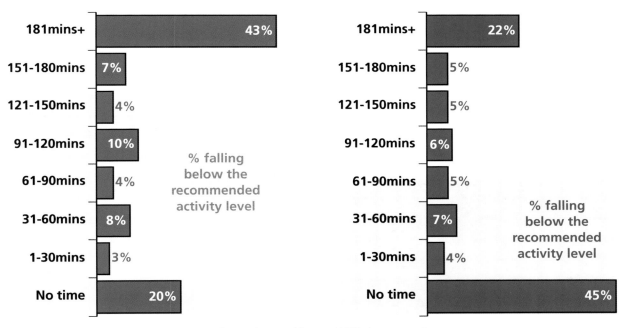

Moderate physical activity?

Time	%
181mins+	43%
151-180mins	7%
121-150mins	4%
91-120mins	10%
61-90mins	4%
31-60mins	8%
1-30mins	3%
No time	20%

% falling below the recommended activity level

Vigorous physical activity?

Time	%
181mins+	22%
151-180mins	5%
121-150mins	5%
91-120mins	6%
61-90mins	5%
31-60mins	7%
1-30mins	4%
No time	45%

% falling below the recommended activity level

NB figures do not add up to 100% due to rounding

Some issues

- Half the people interviewed did not do enough moderate physical activity. How could they be encouraged to do more?

- Even fewer people are doing enough vigorous activity. Why might this be?

- If you want to encourage activity for the sake of health, would it be better to focus on people who are doing some activity or people who are doing none?

How active are women?

Despite recent Olympic fever, British women remain indifferent about sport

The World Health Organization (WHO) recommends that 18-64 year olds should do **150 minutes** of **moderate** physical activity (eg gardening, dancing or brisk walking) or **75 minutes** of **vigorous** physical activity (eg playing sport, running or aerobics) per week.

A YouGov survey of 6,172 adults in five European countries compared results with the WHO recommendations to find out how active women were.

Sources and weblinks:
Source: World Heart Federation
www.world-heart-federation.org

% of the 3,149 women surveyed who...

■ ...DO NOT play sport or partake in vigorous physical activity

■ ...DO NOT meet the recommended physical activity guidelines

UK — 54% / 34%
France — 52% / 42%
Sweden — 47% / 33%
Germany — 44% / 19%
Denmark — 34% / 19%

22% of women in **France**, **18%** in the **UK**, **17%** in **Sweden**, **11%** in **Germany** and **7%** in **Denmark** admit to doing **no physical activity at all.**

"In combination with everyday physical activities... sport can help reduce the risk of heart disease, the number one killer of women, responsible for the deaths of 1 in 3 women worldwide."

Johanna Ralston – CEO of the World Heart Federation

Some issues

• What might stop women participating in sport?

• What might encourage more participation?

• How could school sports be changed so that people continue with them throughout their lives?

Travel & transport

Global road safety

Road traffic injuries are the eighth leading cause of death globally and the number one cause of death for young people aged 15-29

About **1.24 million** people die each year as a result of road traffic crashes.

Between **20 to 50 million more** people suffer non-fatal injuries, with many incurring a disability as a result of their injury.

Sources and weblinks:
Source: Global Status Report on Road Safety 2013 – World Health Organization
www.who.int

Road traffic deaths per 100,000 population, by region

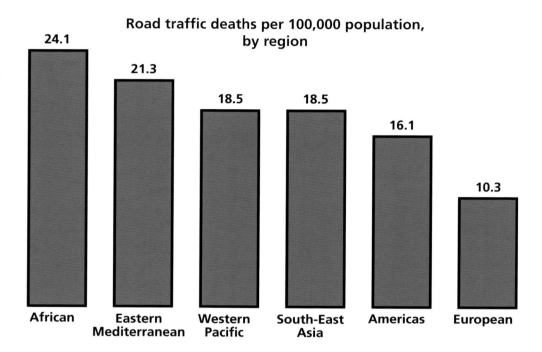

African	Eastern Mediterranean	Western Pacific	South-East Asia	Americas	European
24.1	21.3	18.5	18.5	16.1	10.3

Photo: Courtesy of the Make Roads Safe campaign

The chance of dying in a road traffic crash depends on where you live

Who is most at risk of death?

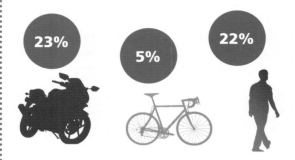

23%   5%   22%

Vulnerable road users

50% of all road traffic deaths are among pedestrians, cyclists and motorcyclists

Age and gender

59% of those who are killed in road traffic crashes are between the ages of 15 and 44 years, and **77%** are male.

Regions

In the African region where walking and cycling are important forms of mobility, **38%** of road traffic deaths occur among pedestrians.

In contrast, in many Western Pacific countries where motorcycles are used frequently, **36%** of road traffic deaths are among motorised two- and three-wheelers.

Income

More than 90% of deaths that result from road traffic injuries occur in low- and middle-income countries.

Even within high-income countries, people from lower class backgrounds are more likely to be involved in road traffic crashes than the more wealthy.

Although middle-income countries have only **52%** of the world's vehicles, they have **80%** of the world's road traffic deaths.

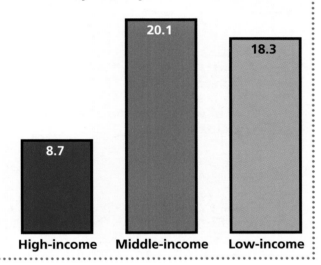

Deaths per 100,000 population, by country income status

High-income	Middle-income	Low-income
8.7	20.1	18.3

Risk factors

The five key risk factors which need to be tackled to reduce road traffic deaths are:
speeding, drinking and driving, failing to use motorcycle helmets, seat-belts and **child restraints**.

Only 28 countries, covering **7%** of the world's population, have adequate road safety laws on all of these.

Some issues

- Can you suggest why younger people, particularly males, are more likely to be killed in road crashes? Would the reasons be different for different countries?

- Can you suggest how country income affects road safety? What about personal income?

- If you could create a world wide law to cover one risk factor which one would it be?

Young drivers

The first few years of driving are a dangerous time – a lack of experience combined with a misplaced confidence can often result in a crash

Every day, 5 people die on Britain's roads and 67 people suffer a serious injury.

19,284 British drivers were surveyed for a report into young driver safety. All the drivers surveyed were AA members.

NB Because of the age profile of AA members, young drivers were a smaller proportion of the survey group than of the general driving population

Sources and weblinks:
Source: Young drivers at risk report, AA Charitable Trust; Make Roads Safe Campaign
www.theaa.com
www.makeroadssafe.org

First crashes

14,229 drivers had been involved in car crashes. Of the drivers surveyed:

- **37%** of drivers had crashed by the time they were 23 years old.

- **28%** had crashed by the time they were 21 years of age.

- **26%** had crashed **within two years** of passing their test.

- **33%** of 18-24 year olds had been involved in an accident when driving and **23%** had crashed **within 6 months** of passing their test

- First crashes were most likely to happen in the day time – only **13%** happened at night.

- Bad weather was a factor in **15%** of cases.

- **47%** happened on a single carriageway or in a rural area.

- **63%** didn't have passengers in their car.

- **5%** of drivers had their first crash on a motorbike.

Unsafe

29% of young drivers said they had friends whose driving was so unsafe they either refused or avoided being driven by them.

Drink driving

16% of 18 to 24 year olds had travelled in a car with a drunk driver, **twice as many** as any other age group.

28% of 18-24 year olds said their friends were likely to encourage them to drink *'one more for the road'* when they were a designated driver.

In 2010:

- Nearly **33%** of car occupants killed or seriously injured were under the age of 25.

- Young people aged 17 to 24, travelling in cars make up **12%** of all road deaths and **26%** of car user deaths.

- The AA estimated that **200** road deaths may be due to drug driving or a combination of drugs and alcohol.

- **30%** of young (17-24) drivers killed were over the legal drink drive limit.

- Nearly **25%** of young drivers killed were **over twice** the legal limit – the highest age group for that figure.

- Driver distraction from mobile phones is a growing problem. Surveys show that **25%** of young drivers admit to accessing email or social-networking sites from their phones while driving.

Education

"By the age of 17 attitudes towards driving will already have been largely formed. If teenagers have had interesting and practical road safety education they are less likely to take dangerous risks when they get behind the wheel alone"

Edmund King,
Director of the AA Charitable Trust

Some issues

- Do you think the reasons given for young drivers being involved in crashes are accurate?

- Why do you think that young drivers are more likely to drink and drive?

- Given that young drivers are so likely to crash and be injured, should there be stricter laws in place, eg should the driving age be raised to 21? Should penalties be tougher for offences?

Distracted drivers

"...taking your eyes off the road for only a second could have disastrous consequences..."

Kevin Pratt,
Car Insurance Expert

Drivers are classed as distracted when they pay attention to a second activity while driving. This may reduce their driving standard, for example making them less observant or likely to make worse decisions about how to control the vehicle safely.

2,012 British UK adult drivers were asked about their driving habits.

Sources and weblinks:
Source: MoneySupermarket.com; RoSPA
www.moneysupermarket.com
www.rospa.com

Drivers were asked if they had done any of the following. They admitted they had:

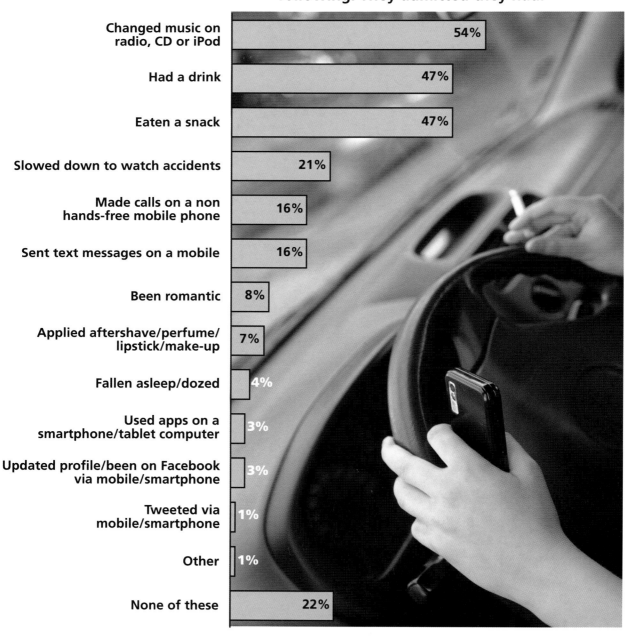

Changed music on radio, CD or iPod	54%
Had a drink	47%
Eaten a snack	47%
Slowed down to watch accidents	21%
Made calls on a non hands-free mobile phone	16%
Sent text messages on a mobile	16%
Been romantic	8%
Applied aftershave/perfume/lipstick/make-up	7%
Fallen asleep/dozed	4%
Used apps on a smartphone/tablet computer	3%
Updated profile/been on Facebook via mobile/smartphone	3%
Tweeted via mobile/smartphone	1%
Other	1%
None of these	22%

Things that have caused drivers to be distracted

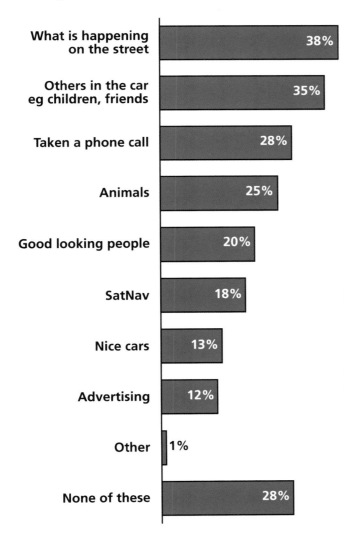

What is happening on the street	38%
Others in the car eg children, friends	35%
Taken a phone call	28%
Animals	25%
Good looking people	20%
SatNav	18%
Nice cars	13%
Advertising	12%
Other	1%
None of these	28%

76% said they'd been distracted while driving, endangering themselves and those around them.

Some issues

- Which of these distractions are avoidable?

- If someone had caused an accident because, for example, they were changing their music, would you excuse them because most people do that?

- Would you make any of these actions illegal in order to increase road safety?

Cycling accidents

Every year in Great Britain, around 19,000 cyclists are killed or injured in reported road accidents

About a **fifth** of cyclists killed and injured are children.

Cycling accidents increase as children grow older, with 10 to 15 year old riders being more at risk than other age groups.

Sources and weblinks:
*Source: RoSPA; Department for Transport
© Crown copyright 2013
www.rospa.com
www.gov.uk*

4 out of 5 cyclist casualties are male

TYPES OF ACCIDENTS

Accidents involving child cyclists are often caused by the child playing, doing tricks, riding too fast or losing control.

For teenage and adult cyclists, accidents are more likely to involve collisions with motor vehicles.

About **16%** of fatal or serious cyclist accidents reported to the police do not involve a collision but are caused by the rider losing control of their bicycle.

All cyclist casualties, 2012

TOTAL

19,091

 **Slightly injured (15,751)**

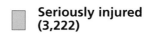 **Seriously injured (3,222)**

■ **Killed (118)**

REPORTED ACCIDENTS

These figures only include the number of cyclists killed or injured in road accidents that were **reported to the police**. The figures also exclude cycling accidents that are away from the road.

Although the number of deaths will be accurate, there could be **two or three times** as many **seriously injured** cyclists and **double** the number of **slightly injured**.

WHERE DO MOST ACCIDENTS HAPPEN

Most accidents happen in urban areas, especially near a road junction. Roundabouts are particularly dangerous.

However, **almost half** of cyclist deaths occur on rural roads.

Riders are more likely to suffer serious or fatal injuries on higher speed roads.

CAUSES OF COLLISIONS

The most common factor in collisions involving a bike and another vehicle, especially at junctions is **failing to look properly**.

This is blamed on the car driver in **57%** of serious collisions and on the cyclist in **43%** of cases.

VEHICLES INVOLVED

The most common vehicles involved in collisions with cyclists are cars or taxis. In 25% of fatal cyclist accidents, the front of the vehicle hit the rear of the bicycle.

Heavy goods vehicles (HGVs) are a particular danger for cyclists, especially in London where around **20%** of cyclists' deaths involve an HGV.

WHEN DO MOST ACCIDENTS HAPPEN?

- About **80%** of cycling accidents happen in daylight. **90%** of child cyclists accidents are during the day.

- The most dangerous hours for cyclists are 8am to 9am and 3pm to 6pm on weekdays. However cycling accidents in the dark are more likely to be fatal.

- More cycle accidents happen between May and September than in October to April.

Some issues

- Most accidents happen in the daylight and in the summer months. Can you suggest why?

- In your own experience, how could drivers change their behaviour to prevent accidents? And how could cyclists change?

- What could be done to make cycling safer and more popular in the UK?

London 2012 visits

The global interest in the Olympics and Paralympics boosted travel and tourism to the UK in 2012

There were 685,000 visitors to the UK during July to September 2012 whose visit related to the Olympics/Paralympics. Most visitors were made by people living in Europe and they were high spenders.

Sources and weblinks:
Source: Office for National Statistics
© Crown copyright 2013
www.ons.gov.uk

470,000 people said the main purpose of their visit was the Olympics/Paralympics

215,000 people visited the UK for another reason but went to a ticketed event

MAIN countries the visitors came from

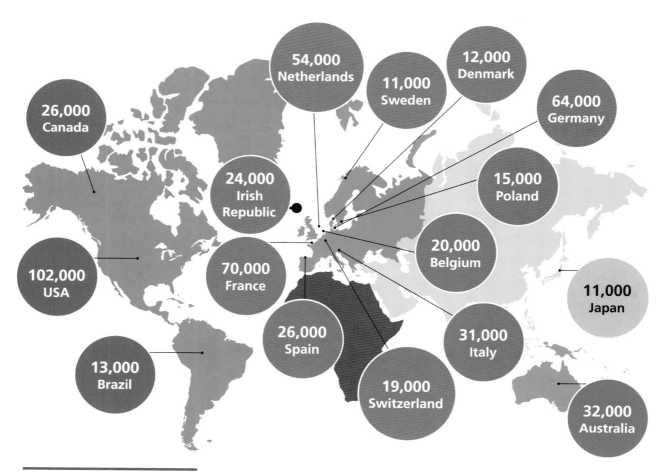

- 54,000 Netherlands
- 11,000 Sweden
- 12,000 Denmark
- 64,000 Germany
- 26,000 Canada
- 24,000 Irish Republic
- 15,000 Poland
- 102,000 USA
- 70,000 France
- 20,000 Belgium
- 11,000 Japan
- 26,000 Spain
- 31,000 Italy
- 13,000 Brazil
- 19,000 Switzerland
- 32,000 Australia

Where the 470,000 visitors stayed and average stay – July to September 2012

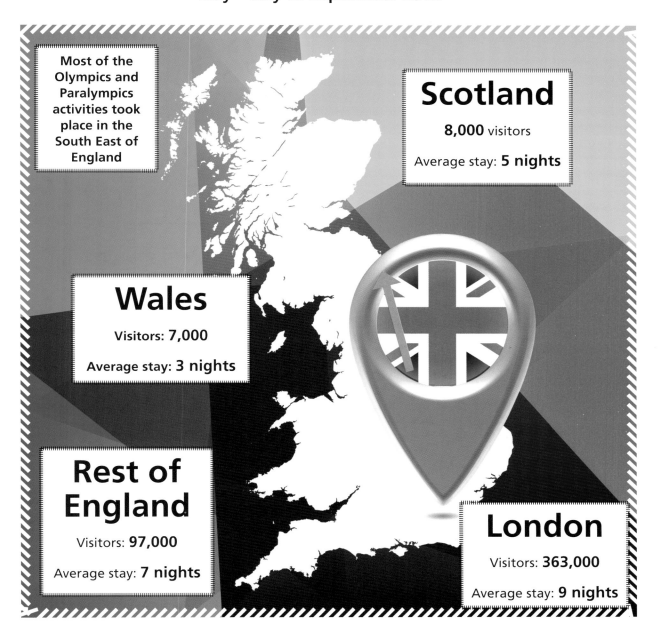

Most of the Olympics and Paralympics activities took place in the South East of England

Scotland
8,000 visitors

Average stay: **5 nights**

Wales
Visitors: **7,000**

Average stay: **3 nights**

Rest of England
Visitors: **97,000**

Average stay: **7 nights**

London
Visitors: **363,000**

Average stay: **9 nights**

Big spenders

Olympics visitors contributed to an increase of **11%** on the same period the previous year, equivalent to **£316 million** in earnings from overnight visits to London.

People who visited the UK primarily for an Olympics/Paralympics-based purpose spent an average of **£1,510** on their visit, double the spending of people who visited for other reasons.

Some issues

- Did the UK in general benefit from hosting the Olympics and Paralympics?

- Do you think the Olympics and Paralympics will have any positive long-term effect?

- Is there an event which would encourage you to travel to a country you wouldn't have visited otherwise?

Holidays

The TripBarometer by TripAdvisor is based on an online survey conducted in December 2012 - January 2013. A total of 15,595 people from 26 countries spanning 7 regions participated.

49% of travellers worldwide plan on increasing their travel budget for 2013 compared to 2012

Sources and weblinks:
Source: TripBarometer by TripAdvisor, MasterCard Global Cities Destination Index, 2013
www.tripadvisor.com
www.mastercard.com

SPENDING TIME WITH LOVED ONES

Globally, the majority of tourists' last trip was for leisure purposes **(68%)**.

People from the Middle East are the most likely to travel with their extended family members **(30%)**, while South Americans are the most likely to travel with their children **(26%)**.

Men are more likely than women to travel on their own (**16%** of men, **12%** of women). Those aged over 65 are significantly more likely to travel with their spouse / partner **(70%)**, while those aged 18-24 are the most likely to travel with their friends **(30%)**.

The vast majority of people travel with someone else **(86%)**

Who do you tend to travel with?
People could provide more than one answer

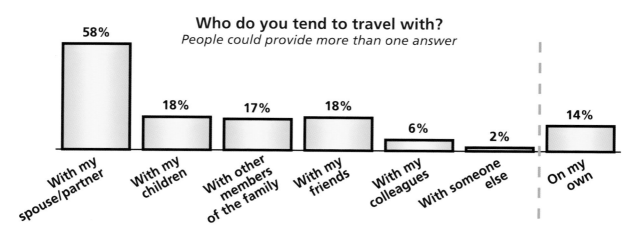

- With my spouse/partner: 58%
- With my children: 18%
- With other members of the family: 17%
- With my friends: 18%
- With my colleagues: 6%
- With someone else: 2%
- On my own: 14%

HITTING THE BEACH AND CRAVING CULTURE

The most popular type of holiday among the 68% who travelled for leisure was a beach holiday. The next most popular type of holiday was cultural.

What type of holiday do you prefer?

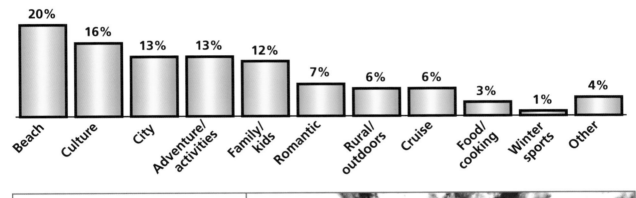

Beach	20%
Culture	16%
City	13%
Adventure/activities	13%
Family/kids	12%
Romantic	7%
Rural/outdoors	6%
Cruise	6%
Food/cooking	3%
Winter sports	1%
Other	4%

SUN, SEA, SURF AND SAND, AND ALSO SOME CULTURE

Travellers from Africa, South America and North America are the most likely to prefer beach holidays (**30%**, **25%** and **24%** respectively), while Asian travellers prefer the excitement of a city break (**16%**).

22% of women and **19%** of men prefer beach holidays and women are also slightly more inclined to be 'culture vultures' (**18%** of women and **13%** males prefer culture based trips).

Not surprisingly, people over 65 years are more likely to prefer cultural based trips (**22%**), while younger respondents are more likely to travel in search of adventure / activities (**20%**).

CULTURE AND CITY BREAKS

Altogether **29%** of people prefer culture and city breaks. A recent report shows that Bangkok ranked as the top city destination for travellers in 2013.

Photo: ajornyot / Shutterstock.com

Top 20 Destination Cities in 2013, by international overnight visitors (millions)

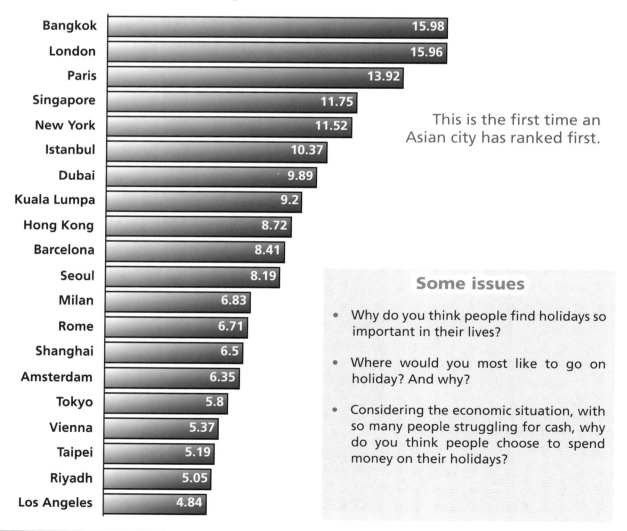

City	Visitors
Bangkok	15.98
London	15.96
Paris	13.92
Singapore	11.75
New York	11.52
Istanbul	10.37
Dubai	9.89
Kuala Lumpa	9.2
Hong Kong	8.72
Barcelona	8.41
Seoul	8.19
Milan	6.83
Rome	6.71
Shanghai	6.5
Amsterdam	6.35
Tokyo	5.8
Vienna	5.37
Taipei	5.19
Riyadh	5.05
Los Angeles	4.84

This is the first time an Asian city has ranked first.

Some issues

- Why do you think people find holidays so important in their lives?

- Where would you most like to go on holiday? And why?

- Considering the economic situation, with so many people struggling for cash, why do you think people choose to spend money on their holidays?

War &
conflict

Forced to flee

The number of displaced people in 2012 was the highest figure ever recorded

Internally Displaced Persons (IDPs) are people who have been forced to flee or leave where they usually live because of armed conflict, violence, or human rights abuses, but they have remained within their own country.

In 2012 Syria was the regional hotspot with a five-fold increase in the number of IDPs.

Sources and weblinks:

Source: Global Overview 2012 – Internal Displacement Monitoring Centre; UNHCR
www.internal-displacement.org
www.unhcr.org.uk

The total number of people internally displaced was estimated to be **28.8 million** – an increase of **2.4 million** on 2011

How the number of people displaced changed between 2011 and 2012

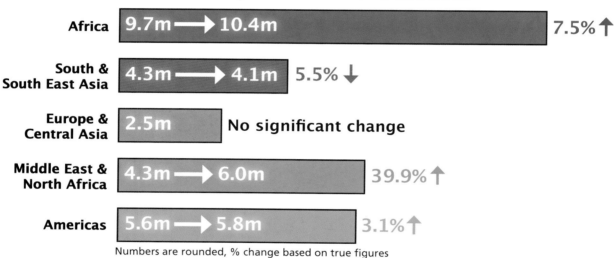

Africa	9.7m ⟶ 10.4m	7.5% ↑
South & South East Asia	4.3m ⟶ 4.1m	5.5% ↓
Europe & Central Asia	2.5m	No significant change
Middle East & North Africa	4.3m ⟶ 6.0m	39.9% ↑
Americas	5.6m ⟶ 5.8m	3.1% ↑

Numbers are rounded, % change based on true figures

The number of **NEW displacements** in 2012 was **6.5 million** – nearly **twice as many** as the 3.5 million during 2011

Where did the NEW IDPs come from?

Africa: 2.4 million
DR Congo 1 million;
Sudan 500,000; Mali 227,000;
South Sudan 190,000;
Somalia 185,000

Middle East & North Africa: 2.5m
2.4m of these occurred in Syria

South & South East Asia: 1.4 million
India 500,000;
Pakistan 412,000;
Myanmar 166,000

Americas: 230,000
in Colombia

Members of a Congolese family fleeing their village.

Photo courtesy of UNHCR / M. Sibiloni / July 2012

How many returned home?

Only **2.1 million** people were reported as having returned home in 2012, a decrease of around **250,000** on the figure for 2011.

Africa: 1.3 million

Côte d'Ivoire 500,000;
DR Congo 450,000;
Sudan 91,000; Chad 36,000

Middle East & North Africa: 550,000

Iraq 213,000; Libya 190,000;
Yemen 134,000

South & South East Asia: 261,000

Philippines 157,000;
Pakistan 59,000;

Europe & Central Asia: 1,600

Countries with the largest number of displacements, 2012

Colombia: Between 4.9 – 5.5 million

Syria: 3 million

DR Congo: 2.7 million

Sudan: 2.2 million

Iraq: 2.1 million

Somalia: Between 1.1 – 1.36 million

Some issues

- When people have to flee their homes, where should they turn for help?

- Why do so few people return home?

See also Essential Articles 2014, A typical day in the life of an internally displaced person in Mali, p186

Civilian casualties

Civilians are increasingly the victims when explosive weapons are used

58 separate countries or territories were directly affected by explosive violence in 2012.

The actual number of civilians killed and injured by bombs and shells is likely to be far higher than the figures shown but this data is an indicator of the scale and impact of the violence.

Sources and weblinks:
Source: An Explosive Situation
© Action on Armed Violence 2013
www.aoav.org.uk

Top 10 countries and territories with the highest reported number of civilian casualties from explosive violence

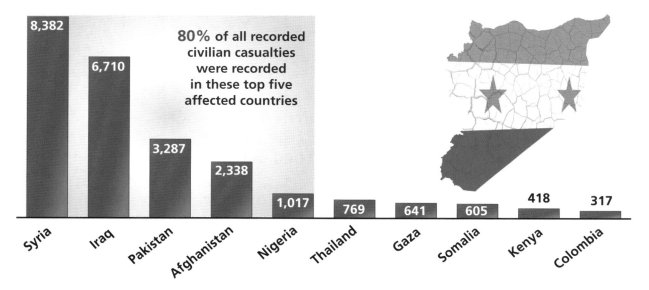

80% of all recorded civilian casualties were recorded in these top five affected countries

Syria	Iraq	Pakistan	Afghanistan	Nigeria	Thailand	Gaza	Somalia	Kenya	Colombia
8,382	6,710	3,287	2,338	1,017	769	641	605	418	317

Photo: fpolat69 / Shutterstock.com

SYRIA

- Syria was the worst affected country in the world in 2012 for explosive violence. **91%** of all casualties were civilians.

- There were **23%** more casualties from explosive weapons in Syria than Iraq, the 2nd most affected country in the world.

- There were **427** incidents which amounted to **20** casualties on average, per incident.

Numbers killed and injured in explosive attacks

Since 2011, there has been a **26%** increase in the number of civilians who were killed or wounded by explosive weapons such as tank shells, mortars, car bombs, landmines and grenades.

34,758 people were killed and injured by explosive weapons in **2,742** incidents.

78% of those affected – **27,025** people – were civilians. The remainder were casualties from armed groups such as military personnel, police, security guards, intelligence officers and paramilitary forces.

Of all worldwide incidents where we know the age of the casualty, **15%** of civilian casualties were children.

The civilian casualty rate depends on the area targeted

Civilian casualties by area of attack	
Populated areas	Non-populated areas
1,674 attacks	**1,068** attacks
91% were civilian casualties	**32%** were civilian casualties

Location of attack	Total casualties	% of civilian casualties	Average civilian casualties per attack
Markets	2,905	93%	25
Urban residential areas	2,868	91%	9
Places of worship	1,950	94%	23

A child passes a bombed-out residential block in Gaza City

Photo: Ryan Rodrick Beiler / Shutterstock.com

Site of a car bomb blast at a market in Pakistan

Photo: Asianet-Pakistan / Shutterstock.com

The civilian casualty rate also depended on the type of explosive weapon used

Improvised explosive devices (IEDs)
eg homemade and makeshift bombs

16,933 civilians killed and injured

60% of incidents happened
in populated areas
91% of casualties in these areas
were civilians
62.7% of all civilian casualties were
caused by IEDs
26 casualties on average
were caused by car bombs

Ground-launched explosive weapons
eg shelling and grenade attacks

6,808 civilians killed and injured

80% of incidents happened
in populated areas
93% of casualties in these areas
were civilians
25.2% of all civilian casualties were
caused by ground-launched weapons
9 casualties on average were caused
by mortars and **6** by grenades

Air-launched explosive weapons
eg weapons fired and dropped
from aircraft

2,518 civilians killed and injured

50% of incidents happened
in populated areas
86% of casualties in these areas
were civilians
9.3% of all civilian casualties were
caused by air-launched weapons
14 casualties on average
were caused by air-dropped bombs

Some issues

- Why are these figures estimates rather than an accurate count?

- Can you find reasons why the number of civilians injured in attacks has increased?

- Is there any way to protect innocent people from involvement in conflicts?

Wider world

World poverty

A new way of measuring poverty shows that some of the poorest people in the world are likely to see some improvements

The Multidimensional Poverty Index (MPI) calculates poverty by looking at different types of deprivation – health, education and living standards – not just income

The 2013 MPI covers 104 countries. This amounts to around **5.4 billion** people – **1.6 billion** of whom are living in poverty measured by these types of deprivation.

Sources and weblinks:
Source: Multidimensional Poverty Index 2013, Oxford Poverty & Human Development Initiative
www.ophi.org.uk

People are classed as multidimensionally poor if they are deprived in one third or more of the following ten indicators

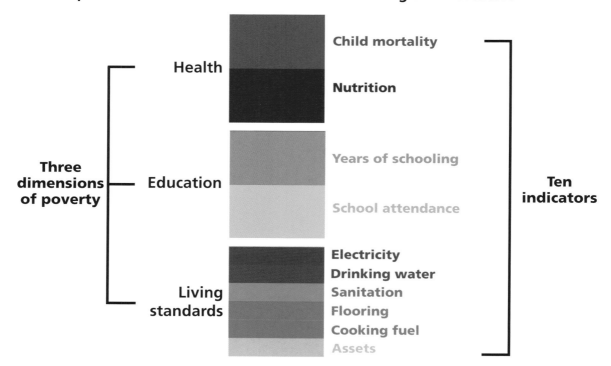

Three dimensions of poverty

- Health
  - Child mortality
  - Nutrition
- Education
  - Years of schooling
  - School attendance
- Living standards
  - Electricity
  - Drinking water
  - Sanitation
  - Flooring
  - Cooking fuel
  - Assets

Ten indicators

Examples of deprivation in family or household

- **Child Mortality:** Any child in the family has died.

- **Nutrition:** Any adult or child, for whom there is nutritional information, is malnourished.

- **Years of schooling:** No household member has completed five years of schooling.

- **School attendance:** Any school-aged child is not attending school in years 1 to 8.

- **Electricity:** Household has no electricity.

- **Drinking water:** Household lacks access to clean drinking water or clean water is more than a 30-minute walk from home, round-trip.

- **Sanitation:** Household does not have adequate sanitation or their toilet is shared.

- **Flooring:** Household has a dirt, sand or dung floor.

- **Cooking fuel:** deprived if the household cooks with wood, charcoal or dung.

- **Assets:** Household does not own more than one of the following: radio, TV, telephone, bike, motorbike or refrigerator and does not own a car or tractor.

africa924 / Shutterstock.com

Best performers

22 countries were analysed for changes in MPI poverty over time. **18** reduced poverty significantly.

The biggest absolute reductions in MPI poverty were seen in countries with relatively high poverty levels. **Nepal, Rwanda and Bangladesh** were the top performers, followed by Ghana, Tanzania, Cambodia and Bolivia.

If progress continues at the same rate, this sort of poverty will be halved in less than **10 years** and will disappear completely within **20 years** in **Nepal, Rwanda and Bangladesh**.

Slower progress is being made in countries like **Ethiopia** where it will take **45 years** to halve multidimensional poverty. **India** will need **41 years** and **Malawi** will need **74 years**.

Best performing countries:
% of people who are poor and deprived in the following indicators
(% have been rounded)

| ■ Child Mortality | ■ Schooling | ■ Electricity | ■ Sanitation | ■ Cooking fuel |
| ■ Nutrition | ■ Attendance | ■ Drinking water | ■ Flooring | ■ Assets |

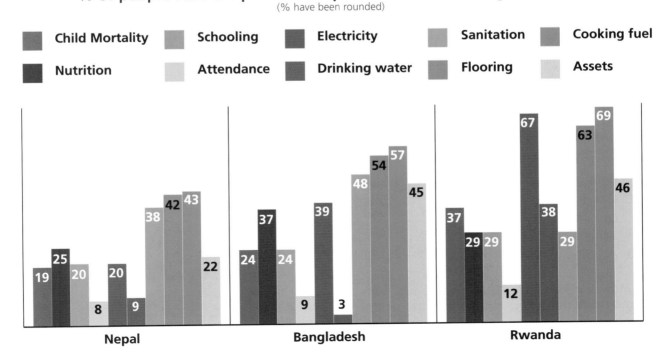

19 25 20 8 20 9 38 42 43 22
Bangladesh: 24 37 24 9 39 3 48 54 57 45
Rwanda: 37 29 29 12 67 38 29 63 69 46

Where do the poorest billion people actually live?
The question can be answered in three different ways:

National level

The bottom billion people are concentrated in **30 countries**, but the situation varies greatly from one area to another within a given country.

Subnational level

The bottom billion are spread across 265 regions in **44 countries**, including the 30 countries at national level.

Individual level

This is the most precise method. Measured in this way, the poorest billion are distributed across **100 countries**

Latin America & Caribbean (1.4%)

Arab States (1.8%)

Europe & Central Asia (0.2%)

East Asia & Pacific (12.3%)

South Asia (51.6%)

Sub-Saharan Africa (32.7%)

Nearly **40%** of the bottom billion live in **India**.

Surprisingly, over **9%** of the bottom billion live in upper Middle Income Countries.

A further **41,000** of the bottom billion live in five High Income Countries:

- Croatia
- Estonia
- United Arab Emirates
- Trinidad and Tobago
- Czech Republic

Once it is known **where** people are poor and **how** they are poor, targets such as the Millennium Development Goals and other goals after 2015, can be successfully met.

Some issues

- Are the ten indicators an accurate measure of poverty?

- Are there any other things you think should be considered?

- How could progress out of poverty be speeded up?

Child wellbeing

A league table of child wellbeing measures and compares progress for children across the developed world

Research in 2007, which looked at the wellbeing of children and young people in some of the world's richest countries, saw the UK at the bottom of the league table.

A new study in 2013, shows the UK now ranks 16th out of 29 countries, but that improvement is not consistent across all areas of life.

Sources and weblinks:

Source: Child wellbeing in rich countries © United Nations Children's Fund (UNICEF), April 2013
www.unicef.org.uk

The 5 dimensions used to produce the league table of results:

Dimension 1: Material wellbeing

– monetary deprivation (relative child poverty rate; relative child poverty gap)
– material deprivation (child deprivation rate; low family wealth rate)

Dimension 2: Health & safety

– health at birth (infant mortality rate; low birth weight rate)
– preventive health (immunisation rate)
– childhood mortality (ages 1–19)

Dimension 3: Education

– participation rate in early childhood education; further education; numbers of 15–19 year olds not in education, employment or training
– achievement (average scores in reading, maths and science)

Dimension 4: Behaviours & risks

– health behaviours (being overweight; eating fruit; eating breakfast; taking exercise)
– risk behaviours (teenage pregnancy rate; smoking; alcohol; drugs)
– exposure to violence (bullying; fighting)

Dimension 5: Housing & environment

– housing (persons per room; multiple housing problems)
– environmental safety (homicide rate; air pollution)

The table below ranks the 29 countries according to the overall wellbeing of their children.

Each country's overall rank is based on its average ranking for the five dimensions.

Key:

| Ranked 1st to 10th | Ranked 11th to 20th | Ranked 21st to 29th |

Rank	Country	OVERALL wellbeing average rank	Material wellbeing rank	Health & safety rank	Education rank	Behaviours and risks rank	Housing & environment rank
1	Netherlands	2.4	1	5	1	1	4
2	Norway	4.6	3	7	6	4	3
3	Iceland	5	4	1	10	3	7
4	Finland	5.4	2	3	4	12	6
5	Sweden	6.2	5	2	11	5	8
6	Germany	9	11	12	3	6	13
7	Luxembourg	9.2	6	4	22	9	5
8	Switzerland	9.6	9	11	16	11	1
9	Belgium	11.2	13	13	2	14	14
10	Ireland	11.6	17	15	17	7	2
11	Denmark	11.8	12	23	7	2	15
12	Slovenia	12	8	6	5	21	20
13	France	12.8	10	10	15	13	16
14	Czech Rep	15.2	16	8	12	22	18
15	Portugal	15.6	21	14	18	8	17
16	UK	15.8	14	16	24	15	10
17	Canada	16.6	15	27	14	16	11
18	Austria	17	7	26	23	17	12
19	Spain	17.6	24	9	26	20	9
20	Hungary	18.4	18	20	8	24	22
21	Poland	18.8	22	18	9	19	26
22	Italy	19.2	23	17	25	10	21
23	Estonia	20.8	19	22	13	26	24
24	Slovakia	20.8	25	21	21	18	19
25	Greece	23.4	20	19	28	25	25
26	USA	24.8	26	25	27	23	23
27	Lithuania	25.2	27	24	19	29	27
28	Latvia	26.4	28	28	20	28	28
29	Romania	28.6	29	29	29	27	29

Lack of data means that the following countries could not be included: Australia, Bulgaria, Chile, Cyprus, Israel, Japan, Malta, Mexico, New Zealand, the Republic of Korea, and Turkey.

How does the UK measure up?

86% of children living in the UK reported a high level of life satisfaction...

...but there is still a long way to go:

- The UK still has the lowest rate of young people going into further education among the countries in the study.

  The proportion of young people age 15 to 19 enrolled in schools and colleges is more than 80% in every major developed nation, except the UK where the rate is just 74%.

- We were placed in the bottom third of the infant mortality league table.

  The UK death rate of infants under the age of 1 is approximately double the rate of Sweden or Finland.

- We are one of only three rich countries with a teenage pregnancy rate of more than 30 per 1,000.
- And we have one of the highest alcohol abuse rates by young people.

  Around one in five children in the UK age 11 to 15 report having been drunk on at least two occasions.

BUT it's not all bad news:

- We have one of the lowest rates of child deprivation in the developed world.

  This means that children in the UK generally have the material things they need to enjoy life – including at least one meal a day with meat, chicken, fish (or a vegetarian equivalent); enough money to join in with school trips and events; the chance to take part in regular leisure activities like swimming; access to an internet connection; and two pairs of shoes that fit properly.

- We are one of only four rich countries to see a drop in the percentage of overweight children in the first decade of the new millennium (the others being Belgium, France and Spain).

- We have one of the lowest children's cigarette smoking rates in the rich world.

  The UK is also one of only four countries that have more than halved the proportion of young people who smoke cigarettes over the first 10 years of the 21st century.

Some issues

- Can you see why countries like Portugal and Ireland, which rank lower for material wellbeing, arrive at a higher position in the league table than the UK?

- Are you surprised that the United States is almost at the bottom?

- Why do you think that might be?

- What is it that makes you feel most satisfied with your life?

Social progress

An index reveals where countries need to improve

The Social Progress Index (SPI) measures the extent to which countries provide for the social and environmental needs of their citizens.

It assesses 50 countries based on 52 indicators covering three areas:

- Basic human needs;
- Wellbeing;
- Opportunity.

Sources and weblinks:
Source: Social Progress Imperative
www.socialprogressimperative.org

Social Progress Index

Basic human needs	Foundations of wellbeing	Opportunity
Nutrition and basic medical care eg undernourishment, food deficit, maternal mortality rate, stillbirth rate, child mortality rate, prevalence of tuberculosis	**Access to basic knowledge** eg adult literacy rate, primary & secondary school enrolment, girls' average years in school	**Personal rights** eg Political rights, freedom of speech, freedom of assembly/association, private property rights, women's property rights
Air, water & sanitation eg deaths from indoor and outdoor air pollution, access to piped water, rural/urban access to improved water source, access to improved sanitation facilities and wastewater treatment	**Access to Information and communication** eg mobile phone subscriptions, internet users, fixed broadband subscriptions, press freedom index	**Access to higher education** eg college/university enrolment, female college/ university enrolment
Shelter eg satisfaction with housing, access to electricity	**Health and wellness** eg life expectancy, obesity, cancer death rate, deaths from cardiovascular disease, diabetes and HIV, availability of quality healthcare	**Personal freedom and choice** eg basic religious freedoms, contraceptive prevalence, access to childcare, freedom over life choices
Personal safety eg homicide rate, level of violent crime, perceived criminality, political terror	**Ecosystem sustainability** eg ecological footprint, CO2 emissions per capita, energy use, water withdrawals	**Equality and inclusion** eg tolerance for immigrants and homosexuals, women treated with respect, community safety net, equality of opportunity for ethnic minorities

Social Progress overall ranking and score out of 100

Ten BEST performing countries

Sweden (1st)	64.81
UK (2nd)	63.41
Switzerland (3rd)	63.28
Canada (4th)	62.63
Germany (5th)	62.47
USA (6th)	61.56
Australia (7th)	61.26
Japan (8th)	61.01
France (9th)	60.70
Spain (10th)	60.43

Ten WORST performing countries

Ghana (41st)	42.69
Bangladesh (42nd)	39.59
India (43rd)	39.51
Senegal (44th)	39.30
Kenya (45th)	38.98
Rwanda (46th)	36.29
Mozambique (47th)	36.20
Uganda (48th)	35.91
Nigeria (49th)	33.39
Ehtiopia (50th)	32.13

UK

The UK ranked 6th in **Basic human needs**, ranked 2nd in **Foundations of wellbeing** and ranked 5th in **Opportunity**.

Many rich nations performed poorly on some indicators

The **US** ranked 11th in terms of **health and wellness**.

Australia ranked 22nd for **shelter**.

Spain ranked 22nd for **personal freedom and choice**.

Many poorer nations performed better than expected based on their level of income

Rwanda was 46th overall but ranked 9th in terms of **primary school enrolment**.

Mozambique was 47th overall but ranked 14th in terms of **equality and inclusion**.

The bottom countries score especially well in **Opportunity**, particularly **personal rights**, **equality and inclusion**, but very poorly in **Basic human needs**. Eight out of ten of the bottom countries are in Africa.

Some issues

- The top ten countries on this index are all high-income countries. Can you explain this?

- This index does not look at the wealth of a country or of individuals. Should it?

- What is the best thing about living in the UK compared to other countries you know about?

Our ageing world

The number of older people in the world is growing faster than any other age group

Within 10 years, there will be **one billion older people** worldwide.

By 2050, for the first time, there will be more older people than children under 15.

Sources and weblinks:

Source: Ageing in the Twenty-First Century: A Celebration and A Challenge, UNFPA & HelpAge International
www.unfpa.org
www.helpage.org

Who is old?

The United Nations uses an age of 60 years old to refer to older people.

Nearly **58 million** people turn 60 each year worldwide – equivalent to almost **two people every second**.

What is ageing?

A population is classed as ageing when older people become a larger proportion of the total population than other age groups.

Why is the world ageing?

A decline in fertility rates, increased life expectancy for babies born now and increasing survival at older ages.

% of world population aged 60 years or over

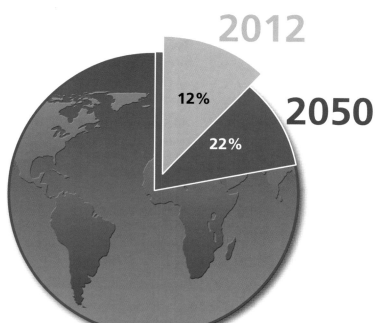

2012

2050

12%

22%

In 2012

810 MILLION people were aged 60 or over

by 2050,
the number will reach

TWO BILLION

" *Today's young people will be part of the 2 billion-strong population of older persons in 2050.* "

Dr Osotimehin
UNFPA Executive Director

Populations all over the world are getting older

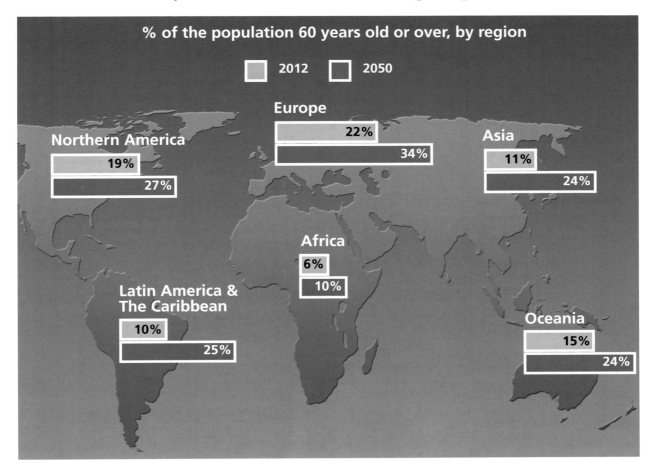

% of the population 60 years old or over, by region

2012   2050

Northern America
- 19%
- 27%

Europe
- 22%
- 34%

Asia
- 11%
- 24%

Latin America & The Caribbean
- 10%
- 25%

Africa
- 6%
- 10%

Oceania
- 15%
- 24%

Life expectancy

People now live longer because of improved nutrition, sanitation, medical advances, health care, education and economic well-being.

In **2010-2015** life expectancy is **78 years** in **developed** regions and **68 years** in **developing** regions.

By **2045-2050** newborns can expect to live to **83 years** in **developed** regions and **74 years** in **developing** regions.

Gender

Globally, women make up the majority of older people.

In 2012, for every **100 women** aged 60 or over worldwide, there were just **84 men.**

Some issues

- Why is the highest percentage of older people likely to be in Europe?

- What are the challenges of an ageing population?

- Are there any advantages for a country in having an older population?

- Can you explain the gender difference?

Challenges

There are questions about whether countries can cope with a growing number of older people. A higher proportion of older people in the population usually means more demands placed on caring and social services but with a smaller working population.

The world in 2100

In 2013 the world population reached 7.16 billion. Even assuming the average number of children a woman would have during her reproductive years (fertility rate) continues to decline, the world population is still expected to reach 10.85 billion in 2100.

Between 2013 and 2100, just eight countries are expected to account for over half of the world's projected population increase

Sources and weblinks:
Source: World Population Prospects: 2012 revision - United Nations Department of Economic and Social Affairs/Population Division
www.un.org/en/development/desa/population

The 10 countries with the highest estimated populations in the world in 2100 and increase from 2013

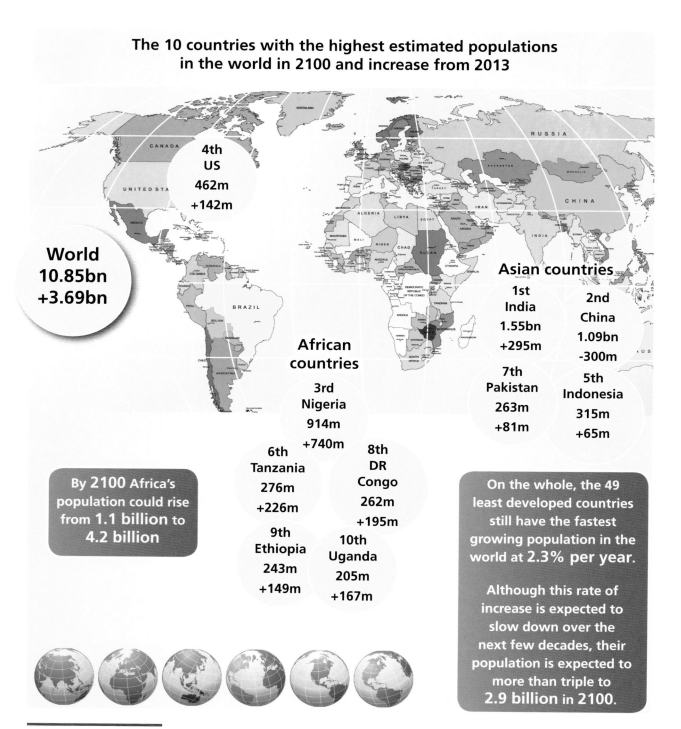

4th
US
462m
+142m

World
10.85bn
+3.69bn

Asian countries

1st
India
1.55bn
+295m

2nd
China
1.09bn
-300m

7th
Pakistan
263m
+81m

5th
Indonesia
315m
+65m

African countries

3rd
Nigeria
914m
+740m

6th
Tanzania
276m
+226m

8th
DR Congo
262m
+195m

9th
Ethiopia
243m
+149m

10th
Uganda
205m
+167m

By 2100 Africa's population could rise from 1.1 billion to 4.2 billion

On the whole, the 49 least developed countries still have the fastest growing population in the world at 2.3% per year.

Although this rate of increase is expected to slow down over the next few decades, their population is expected to more than triple to 2.9 billion in 2100.

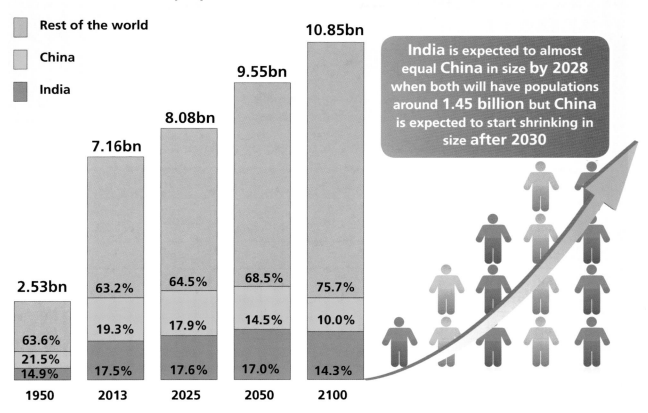

In 2013, 37% of the world's population lived in China and India.

Global population compared to the proportion who live in India and China

- Rest of the world
- China
- India

10.85bn

India is expected to almost equal **China** in size **by 2028** when both will have populations around **1.45 billion** but **China** is expected to start shrinking in size **after 2030**

9.55bn

8.08bn

7.16bn

2.53bn

	1950	2013	2025	2050	2100
Rest of the world	63.6%	63.2%	64.5%	68.5%	75.7%
China	21.5%	19.3%	17.9%	14.5%	10.0%
India	14.9%	17.5%	17.6%	17.0%	14.3%

Average age of selected populations, years

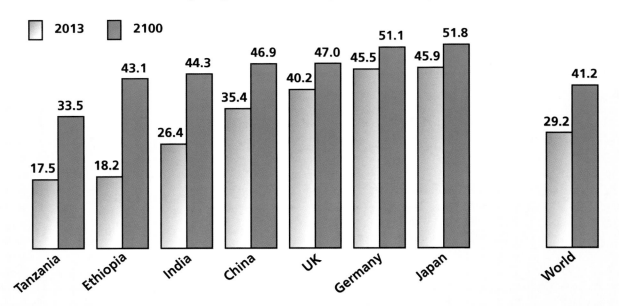

- 2013
- 2100

	Tanzania	Ethiopia	India	China	UK	Germany	Japan	World
2013	17.5	18.2	26.4	35.4	40.2	45.5	45.9	29.2
2100	33.5	43.1	44.3	46.9	47.0	51.1	51.8	41.2

Almost all of the world's additional **3.69 billion** people between now and 2100 will increase the population of developing countries.

Their projected rise from **5.9 billion** in 2013 to **9.6 billion** in 2100 will mainly be distributed amongst the population aged 15-59 (**1.6 billion**) and those aged 60 or over (**1.99 billion**).

Children and young people at an all time high in less developed regions

Currently the population of the less developed regions is still young, with **children aged under 15** accounting for 28% of the population and **young persons aged 15 to 24** accounting for a further 18%.

There are **1.7 billion children and 1.1 billion young people** in less developed regions. This is proving to be a major challenge for their countries - they are faced with having to provide education and employment for large groups of children and youth.

The situation in the **least developed countries** is even more difficult, as children under age 15 make up **40%** of their population and young people account for a further **20%**.

The ten countries with the youngest populations in each year

1950		2013		2100	
Country or area	Median age	Country or area	Median age	Country or area	Median age
Niger	15.2	Niger	15.0	Zambia	27.8
St Vincent & the Grenadines	15.4	Uganda	15.8	Niger	28.4
Tonga	15.5	Chad	15.8	Mali	31.7
Grenada	16.3	Angola	16.3	Somalia	32.6
Paraguay	16.5	Mali	16.3	Nigeria	32.6
Djibouti	16.5	Somalia	16.3	Malawi	32.8
Samoa	16.6	Afghanistan	16.5	Congo	33.2
Fiji	16.6	Timor-Leste	16.6	Burundi	33.2
Vanuatu	16.8	Zambia	16.6	Comoros	33.4
Tanzania	16.9	Gambia	17.0	Côte d'Ivoire	33.5

Developed regions

In the more developed regions, children and youth account for **16%** and **12%** of the population, respectively.

Whereas the number of children is not expected to change much in the future, from **206 million** in 2013 to **202 million in 2100**, the number of young people is projected to decrease from **152 million** in 2013 to **138 million in 2100**.

Some issues

- Is population growth a problem or a benefit?

- Does it matter what the average age of a country's population is?

- What difference does a country's development make to population growth?

Work

Hours and earnings

There is still a gap between the average earnings of men and women in all age groups

The Annual Survey of Hours and Earnings (ASHE) is based on a 1% sample of employee jobs.

All earnings are based on the median i.e. the value below which half of employees fall – this gives the best indication of typical pay as it's not affected by factors such as the relatively small number of high earners.

Sources and weblinks:

Source: The Annual Survey of Hours and Earnings (ASHE) © Crown copyright 2012
www.ons.gov.uk

How the UK employee workforce was made up in 2012

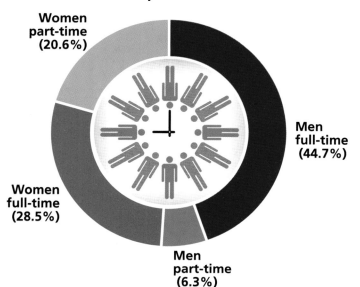

Women part-time (20.6%)

Men full-time (44.7%)

Women full-time (28.5%)

Men part-time (6.3%)

Hours worked

In April 2012 full-time employees worked an average of **39.1** paid hours per week (including overtime).

In comparison, part-time employees worked **18.1** hours per week.

Earnings

The highest earnings per week for full-time employees were in **London**, at **£653** (29% **higher** than the national median).

The lowest were in **Wales**, at **£453** (11% **lower** than the national median).

Median hourly earnings, before deductions (excluding overtime)

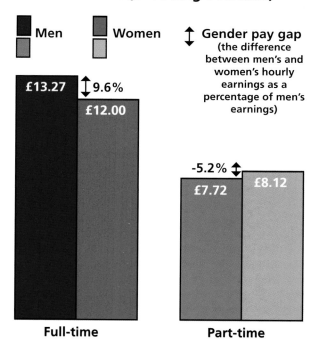

Men   Women   Gender pay gap
(the difference between men's and women's hourly earnings as a percentage of men's earnings)

£13.27   9.6%   £12.00

-5.2%   £7.72   £8.12

Full-time   Part-time

NB Figures do not add up to 100% due to rounding

There were some differences between the distribution of earnings by age for men and women

Men's weekly earnings were highest in the 40 to 49 age group while women's earnings were highest in the 30 to 39 age group

Median full-time gross weekly earnings by age group and gender

Men

Women

Age 16-17: Men £166.70, Women £121.10

Age 18-21: Men £295.90, Women £266.10

Age 22-29: Men £420.20, Women £402.50

Age 30-39: Men £574.90, Women £526.80

Age 40-49: Men £622.30, Women £484.50

Age 50-59: Men £598.40, Women £446.10

Age 60+: Men £509.20, Women £407.40

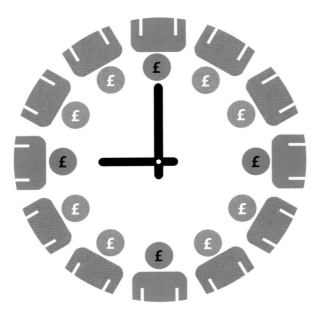

Some issues

- Can you suggest any reasons for the gap in earnings between the genders?

- Some people have suggested that there should be a national average wage which everyone earns, whatever their job. Is this a good idea?

- Why does the earnings gap increase as people get older?

Low work intensity

Throughout the EU, the more people in a household who are not employed full time, the higher risk there is of poverty.

The proportion of people in the UK in this situation, described as having low work intensity, is higher than in most other EU countries.

Work intensity measures the extent to which working age members of a household are fully employed

Sources and weblinks:
Source: Poverty & Social Exclusion in the UK and
EU 2005-2011, Office for National Statistics
© Crown copyright 2013
www.ons.gov.uk

Percentage of people aged under 60 living in households with low work intensity, UK and EU average 2005-2011

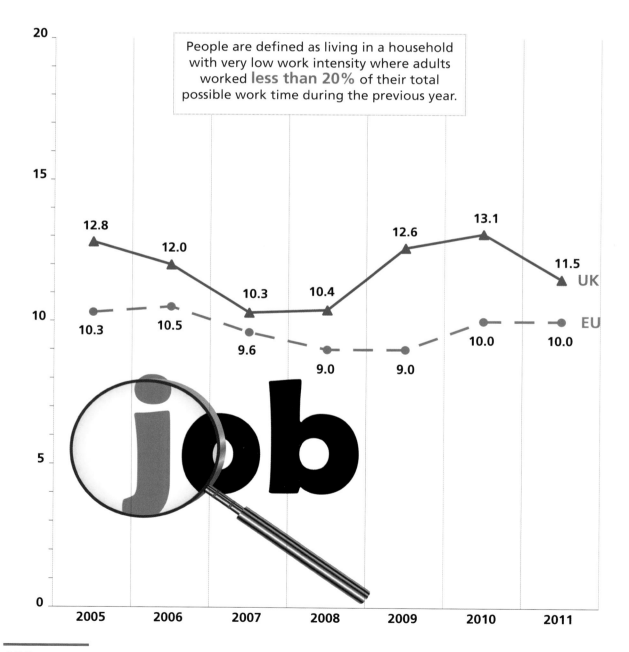

People are defined as living in a household with very low work intensity where adults worked **less than 20%** of their total possible work time during the previous year.

UK: 12.8 (2005), 12.0 (2006), 10.3 (2007), 10.4 (2008), 12.6 (2009), 13.1 (2010), 11.5 (2011)

EU: 10.3 (2005), 10.5 (2006), 9.6 (2007), 9.0 (2008), 9.0 (2009), 10.0 (2010), 10.0 (2011)

Percentage of people aged under 60 living in households with low work intensity, EU, 2011

Ten countries with the highest percentage

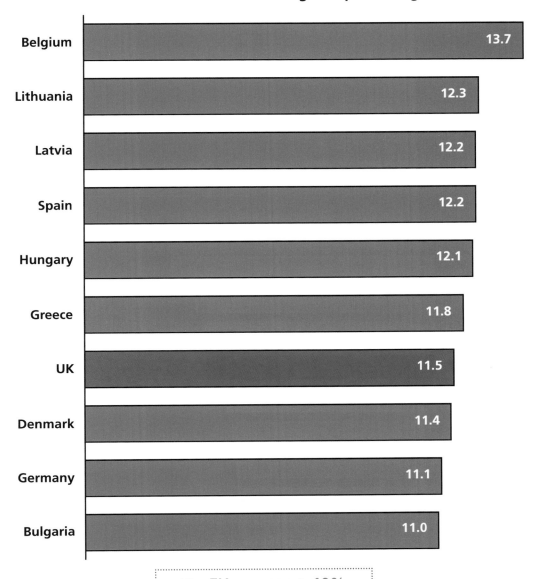

Country	Percentage
Belgium	13.7
Lithuania	12.3
Latvia	12.2
Spain	12.2
Hungary	12.1
Greece	11.8
UK	11.5
Denmark	11.4
Germany	11.1
Bulgaria	11.0

The **EU average** is **10%**

The lowest rates were in
Cyprus 4.5% and
Luxembourg 5.8%

Some issues

- Why do you think people might have some work but not enough?

- Could there be any advantages to not having enough work?

Happiness at work

61% of people overall are happy at work... but money doesn't guarantee happiness

A survey of 2,200 people over 20 professions revealed who was happiest in their careers and why.

Sources and weblinks:
Source: City & Guilds' Career Happiness Index 2012
www.cityandguilds.com

Who's happiest in their work?

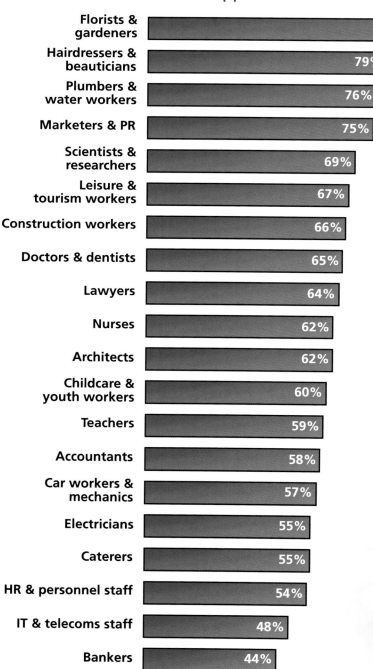

Profession	%
Florists & gardeners	87%
Hairdressers & beauticians	79%
Plumbers & water workers	76%
Marketers & PR	75%
Scientists & researchers	69%
Leisure & tourism workers	67%
Construction workers	66%
Doctors & dentists	65%
Lawyers	64%
Nurses	62%
Architects	62%
Childcare & youth workers	60%
Teachers	59%
Accountants	58%
Car workers & mechanics	57%
Electricians	55%
Caterers	55%
HR & personnel staff	54%
IT & telecoms staff	48%
Bankers	44%

65% of those in skills-based roles were content compared to 58% of those in professional roles

While **61%** of those surveyed said being adequately paid was very important, money wasn't necessarily the key to contentment.

62% of all workers say it's very important to them to feel their work is recognised and appreciated.

What makes us happy at work?

	% agreeing with the following statements	Most likely to agree	Most likely to disagree
I get on well with my colleagues	82%	Scientists & researchers 90%	Hairdressers & beauticians 14%
I feel that I am doing something worthwhile and useful	73%	Florists & gardeners 89%	Bankers 35%
I have control of my duties, and manage my own workload	69%	Scientists & researchers 82%	Nurses, leisure & tourism workers 22%
I am doing something challenging and stimulating	68%	Florists & gardeners 87%	Bankers 35%
I am able to use my skills every day	68%	Florists & gardeners 82%	Bankers 35%
I am in a working environment that I like	67%	Florists & gardeners 89%	Bankers 24%
I have a good work/life balance	64%	Florists & gardeners 73%	Bankers 33%
I feel my work is recognised and appreciated	58%	Florists & gardeners 80%	Leisure & tourism workers 37%
I get support in training and development	53%	Nurses, Florists & gardeners 64%	IT & telecoms workers, bankers 34%
I am adequately financially rewarded	44%	Scientists & researchers 63%	Lawyers 50%
I have scope for career progression	41%	Scientists & researchers 65%	Car workers & mechanics 55%
I have flexible working conditions, such as home working	40%	Florists & gardeners 69%	Car workers & mechanics 65%

Happiest workers by region

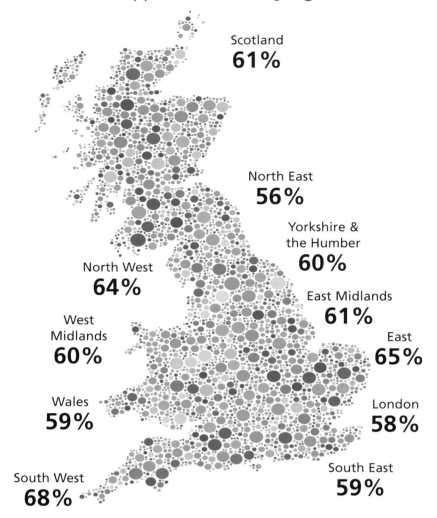

Scotland
61%

North East
56%

Yorkshire & the Humber
60%

North West
64%

East Midlands
61%

West Midlands
60%

East
65%

Wales
59%

London
58%

South West
68%

South East
59%

Happiness by employment status

85% of self-employed people were happy at work.

83% of those who were **self-employed** said they enjoyed having a flexible work life and **91%** said they liked having control over their daily duties.

54% of those in **full-time employment** felt their working conditions were flexible.

54% of those in **full-time employment** felt they were appreciated for their work.

Happiness by age

65% of those **aged 56 and over** were happy in their work compared to:

59% of those **aged 46-55**;

60% of **35-45 year olds**; and

62% of **18-34 year olds**.

Some issues

- Which three statements from "What makes us happy at work?" seem most important to you?

- Hairdressers are among the happiest workers yet they don't get on with their colleagues. What other parts of their job might make them happy?

- Are you surprised that pay comes so low down the list?

See also Essential Articles 2014, International Day of Happiness: Ways to turn that frown upside-down, p122

Shortfall of workers

The UK is suffering from skills shortages across many work sectors

By 2050 the UK will be short of **3.1m** skilled workers.

This is because of an ageing workforce and migration.

Sources and weblinks:
Source: Randstad
www.randstad.co.uk

Demand for skilled workers

The UK will probably have a population of **74.5 million** in 2050. It will need a workforce of **35.4 million** to meet the demands of a population that size.

Ageing

An **ageing population** will leave the UK with only **32.3 million** people in employment, **3.1 million** short.

Migration

This is one of the key reasons for the shortfall. The number of people leaving the country to find work has risen **16%** since 2007, while the number coming to the country for work has fallen **24%**.

The UK has become a less attractive place for the world's most talented professionals and skilled trades people because of its poor economic performance and changes to the immigration policy.

Shortfall in professions by 2050:

Teachers	**128,000**
Construction	**66,800**
Nurses	**61,200**
Qualified Engineers	**36,800**
IT & Tech	**33,300**
Social Workers	**10,600**
Qualified Accountants	**10,200**
Solicitors/Lawyers	**9,500**

Some issues

- Some reasons are given for the shortage of workers. Can anything be done about them?

- When you look at the shortfall in professions, which ones are the most worrying and why?

Index

Entries in colour refer to main sections. Page numbers refer to the first page. Most charts contain UK or GB information.